Deconstructing
Frank Norris's Fiction

Modern American Literature
New Approaches

Yoshinobu Hakutani
General Editor

Vol. 13

PETER LANG
New York • Washington, D.C./Baltimore • Boston
Bern • Frankfurt am Main • Berlin • Vienna • Paris

Lon West

Deconstructing Frank Norris's Fiction

The Male-Female Dialectic

PETER LANG
New York • Washington, D.C./Baltimore • Boston
Bern • Frankfurt am Main • Berlin • Vienna • Paris

Library of Congress Cataloging-in-Publication Data

West, Lon.
Deconstructing Frank Norris's fiction: the male-female dialectic / Lon West.
p. cm. — (Modern American literature: New approaches; vol. 13)
Includes bibliographical references and index. 1. Norris, Frank, 1870–1902—Criticism and interpretation. 2. Masculinity (Psychology) in literature. 3. Femininity (Psychology) in literature. 4. Man-woman relationships in literature. 5. Archetype (Psychology) in literature. 6. Jung, C. G. (Carl Gustav), 1875–1961. 7. Parent and child in literature. 8. Dialectic in literature. 9. Deconstruction. I. Title. II. Series: Modern American literature (New York, N.Y.); vol. 13.
PS2473.W47 813'.4—dc21   96-54247
ISBN 0-8204-3740-9
ISSN 1078-0521

Die Deutsche Bibliothek-CIP-Einheitsaufnahme

West, Lon:
Deconstructing Frank Norris's fiction: the male-female dialectic /
Lon West. –New York; Washington, D.C./Baltimore; Boston; Bern;
Frankfurt am Main; Berlin; Vienna; Paris: Lang.
(Modern American literature; Vol. 13)
ISBN 0-8204-3740-9
NE: GT

Cover design by James F. Brisson.
Front cover art by Alec Pearson.

The paper in this book meets the guidelines for permanence and durability
of the Committee on Production Guidelines for Book Longevity
of the Council of Library Resources.

© 1998 Peter Lang Publishing, Inc., New York

Printed in the United States of America.

To Emily

Acknowledgements

THIS book began as a Ph.D. dissertation written for the University of Maryland at College Park. In the years since Dr. Lewis Lawson, my advisor there, first discussed with me my fumbling, generalized ideas about writing something comparing Frank Norris and Jack London, both the book and my life underwent many transformations. Thanks are due to a number of people for both.

To Dr. Lawson himself I owe much gratitude for his time, patience, and good humor. This was all given both long-term and long-distance, as I lived in first Czechoslovakia and then Oman for most of the time I spent writing and researching the study. Without Dr. Lawson's post-"defense" advice, the dissertation would also not have become a published book.

Living in Prague once again after leaving Oman, I would certainly not have been able to do the practical work of turning dissertation into book without the help of work colleagues and friends—this city, though beautiful and romantic, is not quite the ideal place for up-to-date research or producing "camera-ready copy." Thanks to library director Mike Hubbell and his staff at Anglo-American College, and to my business students Jiri Fryba, Alena Rehakova and Pavel Prihoda's knowledge of computers and English, I managed to do both.

Finally, for the partial focus on psychology and Carl Jung in this study, I have two people to thank. Rustom Bujorjee helped me analyze Frank Norris and his relationship to his own mother and the "Great Mother"—best wishes for health to Dr. Bujorjee, who has had a difficult year. Most of all, though, for ideas, support, Jung research, and far more, I thank (and dedicate this book to) my wife Emily. When I started researching my dissertation nearly five years ago, I was alone; I now have her and our two children to prove once again the power of the ultimate theme both of Frank Norris's later novels and of my judgment of his life and work: love.

Lon West
Prague, Czech Republic, January 1997

TABLE OF CONTENTS

Chapter I Yin and Yang at the Turn of the Century   1
Chapter II Frank Norris and His Time   25
Chapter III The Male Element: Fathers and Sons   55
Chapter IV The Female Element: Mothers and Great Mothers   94
Chapter V Conclusion   120
Works Cited   124
Index   127

1

Yin and Yang at the Turn of the Century

FRANK Norris is remembered in many guises: as a naturalist and sometimes brutal realist who, along with Crane and London, helped kick American fiction into the harsh 20th century; as a young man who needed more maturing but who proved in *McTeague* and in *The Octopus*, his epical attempt to write the "Great American Novel," that he might have transcended his overwrought narrative voice and metaphors to become a first-rank writer; and as a sophomoric racist whose almost Nietzschean display of "man's man" heroes and tall, blonde "man's woman" heroines prove that no additional years of life would have improved him.

These contradictory viewpoints echo the contradictions in Norris himself. He was born in the 19th century and died in the 20th—critics of recent decades have noted correctly that the older century's traditions are his true roots, but he looked ahead to the cold urban life of closed-frontier America as well. He lived both in cultured Paris with its long history, and the new California of the raw-edged American West. His mother was a former actress who read Dickens to him and encouraged—one might argue, too forcefully—both his attempted career as a painter and his successful career as an author; his father was an equally forceful self-made man who probably wished Frank, Jr. only to make money. Elitist and sheltered in many ways, Norris celebrated the most elemental passions in man, and sometimes seemed to revel in the violence of his own fictions.

In fact, the attempt to resolve dialectics—the search for a union between two poles of conflicting perception or experience—seems central to both Norris's life and writings. Many of Norris's critics see this attempt to resolve contradictions as one of the problems of his fiction. A failure to resolve conflicts that few really could resolve—for example, between the harsh realities of the frontier-closing struggle depicted in *The Octopus* and the supremely optimistic philosophy in the novel's conclusion—is seen as evidence that Frank Norris is an ultimately unsuccessful author. Other critics, such as George W. Johnson in his essay "The Frontier Behind Frank Norris's *McTeague*," are more aware of the insoluble dialectic as a theme in, not a reason for judgment of, Norris's work.

Johnson's article shows one form of the opposites between which Norris strove. The East and West of America were a "Great Divide between refinement and strength" (Johnson 94), between the (in Norris's view) effete pseudo-sensitivity of the New York literati and the raw California vitality that he worked to portray in *The Octopus*. Like so many halves of the Norris dialectic, East v. West can be seen as a reflection of the double-bind to his mother and father. When Norris's father disowned him in 1894, Johnson states that he "had to become a man" and end the artistic dabblings championed by his mother. And so, he "faced West" (95)—as, significantly, do the hero and heroine based on Norris and his fiancee at the end of the novel *Blix*. In Norris's view of Romance and Reality, the East, the "great, grim world" of work (*Blix* 278), clearly tilts the Reality side of the scales.

This conflict between Norris's mother and father as influences is not firmly resolved in his work, at least in terms of the sort of figure each might have wanted Frank, Jr. to be. The author's works, both fiction and essays, show admiration of both the strong-willed businessman, such as Cedarquist in *The Octopus*, and the artist. However impotent Presley may often be in *The Octopus*, Norris is clearly sympathetic toward the painting aspirations of his early hero Vandover, and admires the sort of homegrown, strenuous-life authorship he illustrates in characters like Overbeck in the story "Dying Fires," or in the autobiographical Condy of *Blix*. Even so, since Norris himself is so clearly concerned with "masculine" and "feminine" approaches to life—as seen in the three middle novels, *Moran of the Lady Letty*, *Blix*, and *A Man's Woman*, which explore the issue of a good woman's influence in building a good man's character—male v. female is one chief manifestation of the Yin-Yang struggle in Frank Norris.

Although not the author's best novels, these middle or "popular" novels are a good port from which to explore this issue. These three books, neglected or dismissed by most critics, are called Norris's "popular" novels by Donald Pizer because they were all serialized in magazines, and they fit genres—the sea adventure, the romance, the tale of exploration—that suggest Norris was consciously writing to please an audience at this point. But they also probe significantly this central masculine-feminine (mother-father) dialectic. As Pizer writes, one theme of the novels is that the ideal "man's woman" portrayed in their heroines should herself suggest masculine force. By *Blix*, feminine moral awareness plus masculine strength has emerged as the correct balance (*The Novels of Frank Norris* 98).

Norris himself always sought this latter strength as a balance, perhaps, to his "feminine" artistic career. Twice he went to war as a correspondent, seeking adventure and following his belief, noted by his biographer Franklin Walker, that a person must live stories in order to write stories (60). And Norris's battle cry, expressed in various works as "we don't want literature, we want life" or "life is better than literature," is perhaps the key to his personal Yin and Yang. Barbara Hochman's admirably original book *The Art of Frank Norris, Storyteller*, states her view that Norris's "life" v. "literature" is feeling v. knowledge, child v. man, as well as the battling categories of his literary essays, "Truth" and "Accuracy" (13). What she does not say, but which appears blazingly clear in the light of Norris's written beliefs and his characters of both sexes, is that this is also masculine v. feminine.

So in rejecting "literature"—the world of refinement, book learning, East Coast civilization—was Norris rejecting his mother? The entire question of mother (and father) images, relating to the male-female archetypes, and the battling Yin-Yang twins of life, connects to Carl Jung. Popular knowledge of this remarkable psychologist is largely limited to the idea of the "animus and anima," his terms for the essence of each gender as contained within the other. In fact, his "divine pair" of "unconscious powers" (Jung 9.2:21), the animus and anima, is no longer seen as a convincing idea, but the anima/mother by herself, the eternal feminine which both tempts and torments men, is an arresting and fully explored notion that *does* still interest today's thinkers—and though this idea was not yet conceived in Norris's lifetime, it illuminates his own conflict perfectly. This new way of studying Frank Norris's male and female, or more specifically maternal and paternal, characters will be the major focus ahead.

Naturalist or Romantic?

This male/female, life/literature tussle also reflects the literary categories that co-existed as the 19th century gave way to the 20th, naturalism (and realism) in opposition with romance. W. D. Howells, linked by critics to the rise of realism, was also a chief patron of Norris and an influential admirer of *McTeague*. But it was romance that seemed to entice the young writer most. Partly because of such conflicts, although no author can safely be defined under a single title, Norris especially has confounded the attempts of a hundred years of critics to classify him. He was first considered a naturalist, and only in recent decades has he (like his "naturalist" contemporaries such as Crane and Dreiser) been examined outside of this category. Recent critics also tend to see Norris more positively than earlier ones, perhaps because they have freed him from precisely this category in order to examine other thematic facets of his work.

The traits of American naturalism and Norris pseudo-naturalism will be discussed in the next chapter, but one immediately relevant point is how Norris attempted to bridge this literary gap of his time—romance v. realism— by adopting (or believing he was adopting) Zola's creed. A recent critic, Joseph McElrath, describes with some irony the cornucopia of earlier critics' definitions: "Norris was a Realist-Naturalist; Norris was a literary and philosophic Romantic; Norris was a melodramatic, conventional-minded moralist" ("Frank Norris's *Vandover*: Narrative Technique and the Socio-Critical Viewpoint" 27). In fact, Norris probably tried to be all of these things, just as he tried to be both what his mother and his father wanted. Naturalism seemed to him to bridge this gap, as essays such as his "Zola as a Romantic Writer" show.

Critics have begun to realize that Norris did not really understand Zola, and chose him as an early mentor more for the "bigness" of his plots and the forces in them (their "Romance," in Norris's eyes) than for Zola's philosophy. Even his early character-decay novels, *Vandover and the Brute* and

McTeague, are no longer considered truly naturalistic. But this French literary idea did excite him, and in fact the pull of the Old World and the New was also strong in Norris, who was, as his biographer reports, influenced in dress and manner by his youthful Paris experience even after returning home. Like Crane, Norris was using this new theory as a starting-point, but developing it in a peculiarly American way. What Norris always called Romance and Realism in his literary essays is equally a Europe/America dialectic. As Richard Chase famously stated in *The American Novel and Its Tradition*, the American novel is romantic in being freer, wilder, and more daring than the English novel, full of extremes and contradictions rather than unity and harmony (9). Such a description applies well to the works of Norris.

But as romance is presented as a feminine figure in Norris's literary essays, the root conflict remains masculine/feminine. Other expressions of this struggle—domesticity v. wild freedom (itself another form of the naturalistic question of freedom v. determinism) and the major theme of thinking v. feeling—again suggest that Norris saw his parents as representing two difficult-to-reconcile poles. And if those poles seemed to initially draw him in two directions, they must have done so even more painfully after his parents' divorce.

Did the double-bind in fact make it difficult for Norris to grow? Certainly words like "boyish" and "naive" are popular with the writer's critics, and there is an eternal-adolescence quality to the behavior of some of his male characters. Norris's early admirer Isaac Marcosson wrote, "Like Peter Pan, Frank Norris was a wonder-child who never grew up" (240), and whether one chooses to see this fact as positive or negative in terms of his work, in his life this could have had the same tragic undertones as in Barrie's original story. "Could have" are proper words to add, despite the belief of Walker and others that Norris always *was* a child, because the battle was finally won, as in the middle novels (excluding the early *Moran*) themselves, by the world of marriage and adulthood. In the end, Frank Norris did not passively face the "lock-out" from his mother that Peter Pan experienced, but locked her gripping influence out on his own by marrying Jeannette Black. And this progression in the author's own development can be traced throughout his novels.

It is probably not coincidental, in fact, that Norris turned from the sex-as-brutal-temptation stance of the collegiate novels, *Vandover and the Brute* and *McTeague*, to a positive view of romance just as he was stepping out from his mother's shadow to achieve the great romance in his own life. All of the middle novels deal primarily with the male-female love relationship, and how it influences, or should influence, the male partner's development. In part, certainly, this unity of theme may be precisely because the books were written to be popular—in the past as now, to use the familiar, blunt phrase: sex sells. But Norris's love for Jeannette must have made him concerned at that time with this eternally complex, eternally interesting subject.

Also, Norris had always written about sex, but in *Vandover* and *McTeague*, he saw it as an inherited evil, flowing in the veins of Vandover and sending him toward prostitutes and "fast" women, flowing in the veins of McTeague and compelling him, almost against his will, to marry Trina Sieppe. The middle novels stand, in Norris's presentation of women, between this view and the almost goddess-of-love character of Hilma in *The Octopus*. Love is finally fully redemptive in both *The Octopus* and *The Pit*, the first two novels of the uncompleted wheat trilogy. Also, Laura in *The Pit* is perhaps Norris's most complete female character. Thus, whatever their flaws, the middle novels are noteworthy as a bridge between the author's early sexual outlook and his late (and most mature) one.

If sex and violence seem to go hand-in-hand in popular media, they have a clear link in Frank Norris's writing as well. The casualty list in *The Octopus* is the highest, but the most disturbing enjoyment of blood for its own sake as a plot element appears in Norris's first middle novel, *Moran of the Lady Letty*. Brutal details are also cited with relish by the author, again and again, in *A Man's Woman*; yet the main theme of both these novels, as in *Blix*, is the beneficial effect of their heroines on their heroes. How can such material be linked? The author's times provide a clue, for to analyze Norris is to analyze the wars and expansionist desires of his America. Norris can in fact be called "racist," but probably no more so than the average person of his time. He wrote again and again of the march of the Anglo-Saxon race to conquer the world, and his views are even more obvious in the middle novels (as in the moral expressed to an apeman-like Chinese villain by *Moran*'s hero: "Don't try to fight white people") (231) than in such an often-cited passage as the rabbit-killing scene in *The Octopus*, with its "degenerated" hot-blooded Mexicans enjoying the slaughter most. Yet Norris's turn-of-the-century era— the only one in which America was genuinely imperialist in an overseas sense, as the powers of Europe had been for hundreds of years—was one when a naval man could write in a national magazine, "America will be the controlling World Power, holding the sceptre of the sea ... I believe this is the Will of God" (Capt. R.P. Hobson, *North American Review*, Oct. 1902).

Closer to home than the enticing horizons of world conquest, Norris saw the conquest of one part of America—his own West—as a strong illustration of his themes. The subject must have appealed to his belief in his own "marching" race's superiority, to his romantic delight in his San Francisco home, and perhaps to his desire to be as "masculine" as his father might wish. *The Octopus* seems Norris's most evident effort to write this epic, told only so far, as he lamented in his literary essays, by the dime novel and the rightly-called "clumsy, artificial" J.F. Cooper ("A Neglected Epic," *Frank Norris: Novels and Essays* 1202). This was the real image of this chronicle to him: "A scattering advance line of hard-grained, hard-riding, hard-working fellows, Anglo-Saxons, Americans, dash into this country, with its gigantic sweep of deserts, its inhospitable sands, its forbidding mountains, and in less

than a generation have all but civilized it" ("The Literature of the West,"
Frank Norris: Novels and Essays 1177).

Is this view of life as a struggle between brutal men and brutal forces
linked, in fact, to Norris's father? One could argue that his real influences in
choosing man's "animal nature" as a chief theme were Zola and his own
college evolution teacher, Le Conte—but there must have been something
within the young Norris that led these men's ideas to entice him in the first
place. Kenneth Lynn writes that Norris, like other writers of his time, wrote in
a Social-Darwinistic atmosphere "in which everyone competed on an equal
basis—winner take all" and the Alger myth was paramount (3)—and Lynn is
one of the chief proponents of the importance of the father/son relationship to
Norris. This relationship, like the mother/son tie and the characters in the
writer's novels who illustrate it, are exactly what links Frank Norris more to
Jungian archetypes than to Zolaesque naturalism.

Still, as noted, Norris's place in the world of ideas was more in the
century of his birth than that of his death. Whatever his interest in brutal,
"manly" details, he is also linked to the "Genteel Tradition" by such critics as
William B. Dillingham, who gives this tradition the dates of 1870 to the turn
of the century ("Frank Norris and the Genteel Tradition" 15)—in fact the
dates of Norris's own life. Elsewhere the Genteel Tradition has been called an
attempt to create American Victorianism or "veneer of good breeding"—and
specifically in the matter of women, the lesson that "part of their responsibility
in life was to put up with and, if possible, tame the unfortunate animal nature
of man" (Horton & Edwards 191, 198-9).

This is the basis of the "man's woman" theme that fires Norris's
novels. Though one or two voices have accused Norris of writing that a
woman's place was in the home, an invisible backer to her husband—and
though he did himself write such phrases at times—the willful and vivacious
character of his actress mother seems to have kept him from sinking
completely into the cottony comfort of this cliche. The middle novels'
heroines are bold, resolute women, adept at their own careers or planned
careers (sea-captaining in *Moran*, medicine in *Blix* and *A Man's Woman*), and
often stronger than the men they inspire. And yet the issue is thornier than
this, for are these all truly female characters, or are they essentially masculine
beings in the guise of women? This question will also recur later.

But the double-binding influence of two centuries, like that of Norris's
two parents, remains—and it is tempting to see even this conflict in terms of
those parents, with the admirer of Romantic and Victorian novels, Gertrude
Norris, representing the 19th century and the forward-striving capitalist, Frank
Norris, Sr., representing the 20th. There is more to the picture than this, of
course. Frank Norris was subtly molded by the times he lived in, as all
humans are. Johnson and others have observed that the closing of the frontier
was of great significance to the author, and the difficult issues then recently
raised by Darwin and his followers also affected his times strongly. Norris was

no stranger to these issues, having been tutored by Le Conte at college, and God and science are another striving pair in his works. Pizer in fact sees this as his main theme, and Warren French, one of the first critics to see Norris as something other than a naturalist, sums up the appropriateness of this contradiction-obsessed author's dates of life: "Norris stands exactly on the point where the 19th-century faith in the eventual triumph of good curdles into the 20th-century despair at the continued persistence of evil" (140).

To explore these issues further, we need to see the link between not only the parental-influence struggle and Norris's works, but the themes, events, and symbols presented in the works themselves. Sexual urges and violent behavior have long been posited as being closely connected—procreation (continuation of the species) and self-protection (continuation of the individual) as the two great instincts in humanity as well as in animals. What about in the characters of Frank Norris?

Norris's early characters' fear of sex and their destruction in its flame is certainly connected to their brutality. Maxwell Geismar in *Rebels and Ancestors* raised the issue of the connection between sex and violence in his chapter on Norris's "brute" themes. To Geismar, McTeague's sadistic treatment of his wife could have reflected sexual repression, and the sexless heroine Moran in the gory *Moran of the Lady Letty* highlighted a novel that "traced the direct conversion of sexual impulses into a lust for blood" (20, 21).

Probably this is not so much sublimation as similarity—some would say that sexual impulses and blood-lust spring from the same well within us. But Norris may have seen it differently. Certainly the repression of sexual impulses is one aspect of his work; critic after critic has commented on his Victorian prudishness. And if a man's masculinity is no more than an ancestral sewer of desire, as in *McTeague* or the early short stories, then some apparently cleaner, simpler way has to be found to express it—perhaps football, that sport whose physical challenges and "team spirit" Norris found so alluring. Perhaps, instead, an activity similar in many ways to football: war. In a time when Teddy Roosevelt was charging up San Juan Hill, and fighting between Anglo-Saxons and the less exalted race of Afrikaners raged in Southern Africa, there was no shortage of wars to turn a young man's fancy, and Norris, his view of this brutal masculine activity still as romantic as when he wrote his first published work on medieval armor, covered both the Boer and Cuban wars as a journalist. "Somewhere deep down in the heart of every Anglo-Saxon lies the predatory instinct of his Viking ancestors—an instinct that a thousand years of respectability and tax-paying have not quite succeeded in eliminating," Norris wrote in *Moran of the Lady Letty* (74). This simplification of the popular man's-brute-background theories of evolution he heard in his college classroom, combined with praise for his own race's power, is a common theme in his writings.

This interest in violently adventurous outer-world experiences could, of course, be another expression of Norris's many-faceted Yin and Yang—that is, shelter (his own upper-class youthful life) v. the force-clashing world of what he saw as passion and romance. Sometimes, as in his definition of Zola and his use of the term in *Moran*, Norris seems to equate romance with violence. What Don Graham calls "the pattern of movement from genteel insulation to primordial experience" (12) occurs in both *Moran* and *The Octopus*, and is reflected in *Blix* as well, with its pitting of indoor bourgeois parlors against the sweeping vistas of nature. But "primordial experience," to Norris, still often meant simple brutality.

Again, this conflict can easily be seen, as in Johnson's article on the frontier and *McTeague*, as masculine v. feminine—the "brute" that conquers Vandover and some short-story characters is not so far from the male expansiveness and power that is behind the Anglo-Saxon march; refinement, the genteel life of Norris's upbringing, is female in nature and opposed to all of this. Did Norris take sides in this struggle? Johnson asserts that he was always trying to resolve the dilemmas of his life and era, to cross that "Great Divide" (93, 94). This may be true, but the issue was more personal to Norris than this general-outlook aspect suggests. The dilemma was central to his life as well, for as his biographer Franklin Walker asserts, his mother's artistic ambitions for him conflicted with his father's business ones, and all of those who have addressed the parental issue since accept these terms. But what their son's own feelings were can be guessed only from the narrative events and imagery in what he wrote later.

Men and Women

There is much to explore in the entwinings of Frank Norris's male and female characters, particularly in the middle novels, which are central in more ways than chronologically. Still, one might well question taking any note of the least-admired novels of a writer who was himself not of first rank. Whatever the flaws of *The Octopus* and *McTeague*, they are recognized by most as, respectively, a notable attempt at an American Homeric epic and a seminal realistic (often called naturalistic) novel. *Vandover and the Brute*, in some ways more vivid and thoughtful than its college-days companion, *McTeague*, is placed in the first rank of Norris novels by some critics; even the often-derided *The Pit* is seen by French and Larzer Ziff as the author's most mature book. But few spoke up in the past for the popular novels, except, on occasion, to call *Blix* a pleasant antidote to the violent nihilism of the "better" works.

Yet Pizer is correct in asserting the significance of these three derided romances. Their exploration of the gender-role theme is part of a continuing development in Norris's writing. For example, the sex-as-hereditary-evil view in *McTeague* is relevant to the lack of sexuality of *Moran*'s heroine and the death she suffers mainly because of a weakness brought about by love; and the more positive view of a woman as man's helpmate and redeemer is seen not only in *The Octopus* but in *Blix* and *A Man's Woman*. And the lovers in these novels, the Nordic women of towering height and their strong, mindless (not a negative concept in the Norris universe) men, are truer results of the author's psychology than a pseudo-naturalist construct like *McTeague*'s Trina, with her supposedly hereditary miserliness.

Also, the issue of violence, important in its relevance to American historical events of the 1890s, stands out more clearly in a work like *Moran of the Lady Letty* than in *The Octopus*, whose bloody events are based on fact. The racial-superiority theme of *Moran*, the jingoism of *A Man's Woman*—how do these connect to the expansionism of McKinley's day, with its foreshadowing of American involvement around the world during the 20th century? William B. Dillingham wrote in his 1969 book on Norris that the author's lifetime was "a time of transition from an older, rougher way of life to an easier existence" when America had finally conquered the frontier (*Frank Norris: Instinct and Art* 85). With the battle lines being rubbed away, at least on the American continent, men feared getting "soft." And against the invasion of sensitive, artistic, and clearly unmanly men, represented in Britain by Oscar Wilde, stood the "red-blooded" writer Kipling, the poet laureate of imperialism and Frank Norris's first literary mentor. In this climate of masculinity, female characters even had to be given male names (e.g. Travis, Lloyd) if their creator wished them to be seen as strong and noble. But why? It is all mixed up, as noted before, with the sexual drive that Norris at first tried to deny.

This link is most grotesque in *Moran*, where the hero conquers Moran's love by literally beating her up—she then says such things as, "I'm just a woman now, dear," for the rest of the book (238). And in *McTeague*, the wish to surrender is pathological; in addition to his oft-cited passage detailing Trina's "morbid, unwholesome love of submission, a strange, unnatural pleasure in yielding, in surrendering herself to the will of an irresistible, virile power ... her perverted love for her husband when he was brutal" (479), he shows her and her friend Maria, whose husband is equally violent, proudly and competitively comparing their domestic wounds. Yet Norris clearly admired his tall, blonde heroines, like Lloyd in *A Man's Woman*, before men's power diminished them. In fact, Norris's love of violent Nordic sagas—he published two well-written English retellings of Icelandic battle epics—must hold a connection to the Viking appearance of his middle novels' heroines.

But the dialectic is not resolved in these novels—in fact it is sidestepped by their conventional romantic structure, where love conquers all in the end. Perhaps Moran, that bizarrely violent, masculine woman, raises more difficult issues than do the genteel-tradition helpmates Blix and Lloyd—but, appropriately enough, it is she whom Norris finally kills rather than uniting her with her romantic hero.

Was there some belief within Norris's striving pairs that masculine must finally *unite* with feminine—that, as he perhaps wished in the case of his divorced parents, a final reconciliation be found to resolve the Yin-Yang struggle? He may have come finally to the conclusion that many 20th-century thinkers have: that our male-dominated, reason-dominated world is causing its own violence and self-destructiveness with its failure to pair the two "genders" fruitfully. Although there is little evidence in the first middle novel, *Moran*, that Norris saw this—completely masculine, i.e. brutal, behavior is presented as the ideal choice for both male and female characters in that book—by the time of *A Man's Woman*, he was presenting (as in the still-later wheat novels) men finally winning their women through vulnerability rather than power. The brute, animal drives so prevalent in *McTeague* and *Vandover* are replaced during the middle novels by the procreative "Mother Nature" ideal best symbolized by the wheat in the last two novels.

The dualism of body and soul is another form of this struggle which obviously reflects on the sexual theme of "pure" v. physical love. In the middle novels, Norris shies away from consummating his characters' romances—only in the last of them, *A Man's Woman*, is there a marriage, but the hero and his wife are separated soon afterward by his grand mission of polar exploration, and there are no hints of real physical pleasure before this. Furthermore, none of the three romances produce children in the course of the novels—a fact whose significance will be explored later as part of the general subject of motherhood.

How does the body v. soul, or spirit v. nature, issue parallel the other strivings of opposites seen in Norris's writing? It is certainly a central motif of naturalistic literature—Charles Child Walcutt's well-known argument about the "divided stream" in naturalism is expressed in terms of the spiritual and physical worlds, as well as of optimism v. pessimism (another of Norris's personal battles). Walcutt reminds us that Emerson, whom French cited as an influence on Norris, said, "Nature is a symbol of Spirit ... every natural fact is a symbol of a spiritual fact" (10-1).

But early on, body/soul dualism, rather than such transcendentalist unity, was Norris's theme. *Vandover*, as many have noted, is an expression of the old Christian idea that man has a carnal (evil) part and a spiritual (good) one. This is connected to what Stanley Cooperman, an early proponent of the Norris-as-moralist view, called "the Puritan flesh-hate and guilt" of Calvinistic determinism in the U.S. Writers like Norris may have used scientific language (or in the case of *Vandover*, a minutely-described degenerative disease), but, influenced much more by religion than by experimental medicine, the American naturalist took "the duality between flesh and spirit, evil and purity" as his creed (Cooperman 252).

But Norris had other, personal influences, such as the teaching of Le Conte, whose quasi-moral evolutionary theories fit into his own thoughts about morality and animal drives, and about man's "animal past" helping him to survive but holding him back spiritually (Pizer, *The Novels of Frank Norris*

16). And so the physical-spiritual battle turns up in the early Norris again and again. In *McTeague* it is (at least after the overdramatized struggle-with-the-brute scene in Chapter Two) a more subtle battle, but the temptation of sexuality, as much as of greed, finally destroys McTeague, Trina, and perhaps even the grasping junk-dealer Zerkow, just as it does Vandover.

Again, the middle novels provide a transition. They have hints of sexuality, however the subject may be hidden in their broader plots; but more significant than sex's mere appearance is the fact that—unlike in *Vandover* and *McTeague*, which were not written for mass-market tastes and thus were more daring in their subject matter—it does not point the characters toward death and destruction. Longing for Trina in McTeague's case, or for a number of women in Vandover's, is the first step downward in their falls. But for the three heroes of the middle novels, who all begin with various weaknesses, desire for the right woman is the first step *upward*. And from here we move to the luscious, lingering descriptions of Hilma in *The Octopus*—a woman who, as burstingly nurturing and procreative as Nature herself, will be the best force in a man's (Annixter's) life, not the worst.

This is not inconsistent, for in the original Chinese concept of Yin and Yang, the feminine principle is the earthy one, and the masculine the heavenly, soul-based one. But Christianity, with its exaltation of the Virgin Mother, made worship of women in Western literature mean worship of the soul (Jung 6: 216-7, 221). Thus Norris, like anyone raised to think in Western terms, reversed Yin and Yang; in Chinese thinking, *masculine* force generates new life. Yin is winter, and the Yang cycle starts with spring (Clayre 202). By finally settling on woman as both an uplifting and a sexual being, rather than a down-dragging temptress, Norris was drawing closer to Emerson's equating of Nature with spirit, and further from both the "flesh-hate" tradition in America and the traditional Eastern image of feminine Yin as shadowed, hidden, passive.

Still another dialectic which seems to place men and women on opposite poles is thinking v. feeling (or acting)—the exaltation of the second impulse over the first being one of the central tenets of Norris's stated philosophy. Norris's own failure in college probably influenced him to reject the intellectual viewpoint; as he never graduated from any school, it would comfort him to decide that scholarly achievement is not important to a person's development. A number of passages in Norris's novels show this repeatedly stressed position. Moran says, "I've lived by doing things, not by thinking things, or reading about what other people have done or thought; and I guess it's what you do that counts, rather than what you think or read about" (*Moran of the Lady Letty* 114). Lloyd discovers her real love for Bennett in *A Man's Woman* after this assertion by the narrator: "She began to feel instead of to think" (192). And Annixter's vigil in *The Octopus*, in which he realizes his own love for Hilma, contains similar words: "He began to think less, and feel more" (868).

But which gender represents which impulse? Though Moran dismisses reading, her father has books in his cabin on their boat. It was Norris's father who sent him to Berkeley, and the son's failure there probably contributed to the decision to disown him. More comforting, surely, to this man who like his character Vandover could apparently not even do sums very well, was his mother's emphasis on artistic achievement.

The problem of the differing ambitions of the Norrises for their son was of course exacerbated by Frank Norris, Sr.'s desertion of his family and divorce in 1894. Such an event would have a central impact on any person's life. But the natural subconscious worry by a child (even an adult one) that the departing parent is rejecting him, too, in a marital breakup was taken a step further by Frank Norris's father. He *did* reject his son, for the settlement after the divorce left only Frank, Jr. without support, not his mother or his brother Charles. Walker notes that Frank never saw his father again after this, and, like Johnson and other critics, states that this event, traumatic for Norris the person, may have been beneficial for Norris the author (88). He was now free to write, and his year at Harvard under Lewis Gates, who also taught Gertrude Stein, started shortly afterward.

Nevertheless, the hurt probably surpassed any possible benefit. Certainly the novels, beginning with the two largely written at Harvard, are far superior to the violent early short stories and the derivative poem *Yvernelle*, Norris's only writing before the divorce. But *Vandover*, a product of that Harvard year, is filled with guilt and sorrow over a father first disappointed by, and then lost to, the novel's hero. Kenneth Lynn strongly suggests, in his chapter on Norris in *The Dream of Success*, that the parental battle over the son's future was a reason for the split itself. Whether this is true or not, Gertrude Norris was certainly the victor in this battle. However, how did this victory leave her son to feel about mothers and fathers, men and women?

If the "thinking" side of the thought/feeling dilemma represents the masculine principle, as one might initially guess, then Norris may have concurred both openly and inwardly in his mother's wishes. The issue is fuzzier, however. Though "feeling" suggests femininity, Norris always allied this side of that particular dialectic with *action*. Thus Lloyd unites with Bennett, one of the novelist's paternalistic man-of-action characters, not only because she learns to stop thinking but because he fulfills this creed of hers: "to do things, not to think them; to do things, not to talk them; to do things, not to read them. No matter how lofty the thoughts, how brilliant the talk, how beautiful the literature—for her, first, last, and always, were acts, acts, acts—concrete, substantial, material acts" (*A Man's Woman* 49).

Before the divorce, Norris was a weak student at Berkeley, sometimes on probation for poor grades; and though Vandover graduated Harvard "by a squeak" (*Vandover and the Brute* 19), Norris did not graduate from either college at all. Yet his mother-backed Harvard months, in which he actively worked to improve his writing, were certainly more thoughtful than the fraternity-highjinks years at the University of California; and Adler, a character in *A Man's Woman*, pleads that Bennett not be allowed to turn from exploring to writing by saying, "Make him be a man and not a professor" (203). It does not seem that either pole consistently represents one parent or the other here.

More simple, again, is the issue of masculine, often violent, physical striving. When Bennett is a "man," in the first chapter of his novel, he is a brutal one. And Norris, whose failed early effort to play football is seen by Lynn as a significant psychological event, was allured to the end by the male-camaraderie mythology of war. Even in his last novel, *The Pit*, military language is constantly used to describe business activity—i.e., his father's sort of activity. Significantly, Norris's attempts to prove himself on a true battlefield, in South Africa and Cuba, also occurred after the divorce. Yet one critic asserts (without evidence) that the South Africa trip was "doubtless paid for by his mother" (Hart, introduction to *A Novelist in the Making* 28)—and she cared for him after both of his glory-searches in war were ended early by fever. Norris's adventurous stories, such as the bloody and almost implausible plot of *Moran*, may have been one way to compensate for all of this.

Yet this author would not finally endorse the survival-of-the-fittest idea. Norris, the perhaps unconscious adherent to the genteel tradition, could never escape the moral viewpoint represented by his mother's New England upbringing, however much he tried to be a naturalist and express the ideas of his father's often social-Darwinist business world. Like Zola, Norris, who wrote in his literary essays of a novelist's moral duty, did not adopt the total amorality theoretically called for in naturalism.

Always, he felt pulled in two directions. Certainly he was trying to please his father, or to show himself worthy of him, both before and after the divorce. But he was trying to please his mother as well. Like Lloyd and Ward Bennett in *A Man's Woman*, or the Jadwins in *The Pit*, Norris's parents were a couple formed of two strong, willful personalities, and the key to his use of these many dialectics in his writing is the double-bind to these two people. Norris often describes his characters as having a "second self" to contend with—probably feeling that he had one of his own.

In the end, there *was* an escape, and it was named Jeannette Black. At 27, Norris was an editorial assistant—one might even say, hack writer—for the San Francisco *Wave*, and, Walker tells us, now thoroughly "subject to the strong personality of his mother," being urged to live with her and dally in polite society (150). He was much like the callow Condy, who himself lives with an invisible mother, in *Blix*—and as in that fictionalizing of his courtship, it was at this juncture, when he most needed independence to realize his personal and artistic potential, that he met Jeannette. *Blix*, though dedicated to Norris's mother, is like an announcement of escape from her.

Zola may have championed the absence of authorial presence from fiction, but Norris's personal concerns are everywhere in his own writing.

And after the dilemma-filled novels written before he found Jeannette, there is a clear effort to find a solution to the double-bind, in his works as in his life. The progression is clear in the middle novels from the absence of any plausible love story in *Moran*, to the junior romance in *Blix* and the image of truly redemptive love in *A Man's Woman*. Norris then takes his search a step further—or higher, in the transcendentalist sense—to find unity in Nature, the Great Mother, in the wheat novels.

Here the question of whether the famous final passage of *The Octopus*, in which the author makes his most impassioned effort to rise above these dilemmas, is plausible arises. Not surprisingly, the critics who view Norris more negatively find his message here that "all things work for good" most absurd. Larzer Ziff, for example, feels this apotheosis is contrary to and avoids "all the pragmatic consequences" of what Norris has presented so forcefully in the plot (268). Others in Ziff's generation attempted to explain the seeming non sequitir at the book's end with theories that Norris was being ironic (though he always professed authorial sincerity) or romantic (in precisely the literary sense that he loudly scorned).

In fact, what this ending—with its optimism, like that in the saved-marriage ending of *The Pit*, so different from the hopeless finales of the early novels—best expresses, if one recalls Norris's distress at being pulled between a host of Yin-Yang divisions, is the wish for a final unity. The "larger view" it professes is one in which small rivals blend together because they are seen from such a great distance—seen, essentially, by the strict-but-benevolent eye of a Mother figure, the wheat. For however much Frank Norris tried to eliminate mothers from his novels, the power of the *archetype*, if not its human manifestation, finally lent its fire to his last two books.

In this, as in other ways, the popular novels clearly are what Pizer first claimed they were: a bridge between the naturalism of *Vandover* and *McTeague* and the natural dynamism or nature-worship of the wheat books. Lars Ahnebrink, one of the few critics of his or earlier times to take positive note of the middle novels, wrote in *The Beginnings of Naturalism in American Fiction* that they represented a transitional period when Norris tried to "find himself" (124). Perhaps he meant this in a literary sense, but it is an apt phrase in terms of the writer's life, as well. When he began *Moran* he was as young, perhaps as childish, as Condy Rivers in the second middle novel, *Blix*. By the time he was researching *The Octopus* (which he dedicated to his wife), he was a married man and successful author who had perhaps moved beyond the conflicts of his earlier years.

Or perhaps not. Though there is a declaration-of-independence quality to *Blix*, and though *A Man's Woman* brings new complexity and perception to his vision of male-female relationships, the primacy of characters based on his mother and father in *The Pit*, and the continued appearance of failing artist characters like Presley and Corthell, suggest that Norris was still doubtful about himself and his relationship to his parents.

Father-inspired characters continued to appear in *The Octopus*, including not only that strong patriarch, Magnus Derrick, but the industrialists, Cedarquist and the huge, imperious Shelgrim. These money-making heroes, worshipping economic world conquest (Cedarquist) or impersonal, amoral "force" (Shelgrim), remind us of Norris's exaltation in his essays of the great American businessman. In "The Frontier Gone at Last" he not only makes his famous comparison of Richard the Lion-Hearted to a contemporary big businessman (either way, a strong father-figure), but sets forth the same message which Cedarquist later delivers, that the Anglo-Saxon will win today not through battle, but through trade. He also notes that business uses the vocabulary of war—an observation he illustrates himself in the pit-as-battlefield, capitalist-as-general metaphors of *The Pit*. And Curtis Jadwin, the protagonist of Norris's last novel, is an attempt at *the* businessman-hero.

Mothers are represented as well—symbolically, if usually in no other way. For example, Hilma in *The Octopus* is more successful as an archetypal mother than a physical one. Though she suffers a miscarriage, she is seen by the narrator when pregnant as "first the girl, then the woman, last of all the Mother ... And with this, with the knowledge that the crown hung poised above her head, there came upon Hilma a gentleness infinitely beautiful, infinitely pathetic; a sweetness that touched all who came near her with the softness of a caress. She moved surrounded by an invisible atmosphere of Love" (973). And her profession as a milkmaid, in which she is first seen, is almost too obvious. She is not only a potentially fertile Tree (her last name) but a "Hill-ma"—a hill of mammaries, a giant breast, often dripping with milk in her early appearances. But it is cow's milk, for she will never suckle a child of her own.

Before this novel, with its heroine who belongs beside Faulkner's Lena Grove in the list of American literary Earth Mothers—before Norris had a wife or a measure of independence from the double-bind—women were respectable as characters only when they were masculine. This masculinity is often represented by height. Flossie, the prostitute who is paradoxically shown as the strongest and most attractive woman in *Vandover*—her name a faint echo of "Flora," Vandover's flower-goddess childhood drawing of idealized womanhood—is "an immense girl, quite six feet tall" (37); and hilly Hilma is significantly described as "tall as a man" (*The Octopus* 759). All three of the middle novels' heroines share this height, but Moran, the earliest and most unfeminine of them, is first described as "too tall," rather than wonderfully tall like Blix and Lloyd. Yet Wilbur, her future mate, sees her as splendid and romantic, admiring (as Norris may have at the time) a woman as strong as or even stronger than himself.

This exaltation of masculine women seems to place Norris somewhere other than in the genteel tradition, but in fact he did seem to believe in its tenets when he wrote the middle novels. The point is that the gently ennobling women that this tradition presented did not win his respect. As Dillingham points out, Norris admired Moran and Lloyd as competitors, not genteel-tradition "helpmates," and thought less of them after they were mastered. "American writers who have reputations for being tough realists often clearly hold this concept of woman as basically so different in temperament and outlook that it is impossible for her to understand and participate fully in the manly struggle of life." (Dillingham, *Frank Norris: Instinct and Art* 88-9).

And so the early heroines of Norris's novels are weakened—or in the case of Moran and *McTeague*'s Trina, finally killed—by falling in love. It is in *A Man's Woman* (despite Dillingham's equating Lloyd with Moran) that Norris begins to see love as a *mutual* surrender, a blending together rather than a mastering. However much he continues afterward to present images of powerful paternal men, the transition that takes place in the middle novels is most importantly a changing view of women—or of women and men together, which is, after all, any romantic novel's focus.

But even in these novels, there is a feeling displayed that to be the best helpmate—the "man's woman" that was Norris's version of the Victorian woman-as-redeemer—a woman should be somewhat masculine. Pizer wrote that a Norris "man's woman" is closer to a "man's man" than to a genteel woman, encouraging her mate's masculinity "by herself representing its qualities" ("The Masculine-Feminine Ethic in Frank Norris's Popular Novels" 85). Thus Lloyd, much less limited and brutal than Moran, still shares the earlier heroine's male name and much of her strength; and even Blix, the most feminine of the three, often plays a simple male "chum" role with Condy.

What about the level of masculinity in male characters? For there is a third type of Norris character beyond the virile men and women he admires. Weak, artistic, or—if we wish to use an adjective in the same category—feminized men (whose profession usually is artistic) often appear. These men, as one might guess after noting the author's fears about his mother's influence, are based not on either of the parents but on the son—Frank Norris himself.

Who are these characters? As noted, the painter-aspirant Vandover and the writer Condy Rivers are obviously autobiographical. But Corthell, the man who tries to tempt Laura away from her husband in *The Pit*, has similarities to other effeminate-artist characters in Norris's novels, such as Hartrath and Julian Lambert in *The Octopus*. (When one sees the couple in *The Pit* as the author's parents, psychotherapeutic conclusions like the ones Kenneth Lynn draws are irresistible.)

Norris is described by his biographer Walker, after the Paris sojourn, as something of a dandy, returning to America "in silk hat, frock coat, spats, a walking stick" and sideburns (42). (One might think of Prufrock with his fashionably parted hair and white flannel trousers.) Similarly, Vandover comes home from Harvard refined, charming, and well-dressed; and Corthell is described as elegant, with slim hands and pointed, Bohemian-type beard (*The Pit* 227). It should be noted, though, that his mannerisms are so affected—for example, saying "one" when speaking of himself—that he may be based as much on a general cliched artist image as on Norris.

More significant, including to critics who have long argued over whether he is the author's representative in the book or not, is *The Octopus*'s Presley. Though he is called kindred to the feminized painter Hartrath by Mrs. Cedarquist, Norris presents him early in the novel as a manly sort of poet, favoring "life" over "literature." Yet he is finally impotent, too mannered and intellectual to rouse the farmers by his anti-railroad speech, failing even when he throws a bomb at the novel's villain, S. Behrman, and doesn't kill him. A Norris-based character who makes the opposite progression is *Moran*'s Wilbur, who starts as a dandified clothes-horse and ends, tutored by Moran, as a properly masculine and (unlike Presley) successfully violent man.

In this area as well, though, the parental conflict always appears. When we remember that one parent wanted Frank to be an artist and the other did not, we can perhaps understand why he veers between sneering at his poet-painter characters and trying to present them as sufficiently strong and willful to please even Frank Norris, Sr. An affecting illustration of this appears in *Vandover and the Brute*. Vandover's father, a capitalist and moral model clearly inspired by Norris's own father, encourages his son's artistic bent by putting a price on his childish drawing efforts: $1 for his first creation, and $5 for "Flora," his first big achievement. "Never for a moment did the Old Gentleman oppose Vandover's wish to become an artist ... " (11) writes Norris, in a demonstration of, more than anything else, wishful thinking.

If Norris's fear of emasculation by art was in response to his father, his discomfort about sex was, many believe, in response to his mother. The prudishness of his writing does fit into the century he was born in; the Calvinist idea that nature is sin is much more a part of his early novels than naturalism's belief that evil is in the *repression* of natural instincts. But there is more behind it than that.

His biographer states that the stern moralizing in *Vandover and the Brute* occurred because Norris was afraid of his own vices, and of his mother's disapproval of them. That is, the youthful Norris did not live purely himself and was no stranger to women, but he was so ashamed of this ordinary behavior that, as *Vandover*'s narrator, he kept abandoning naturalistic objectivity to condemn his hero. And as the mover of the novel's plot, he subjected poor Van to a degeneration that his own weaknesses were not really enough to cause (Walker 97, 98).

And so, in Norris's early twenties, his discomfort about sex led him to write such passages as the famous struggle-with-the-"brute" scene in *McTeague*. When one reads these lines—"Below the fine fabric of all that was good in him ran the foul stream of hereditary evil, like a sewer. The vices and sins of his father and of his father's father, to the third and fourth and five hundredth generation, tainted him. The evil of an entire race flowed in his veins" (285)—it is easy to forget that McTeague merely finds Trina attractive and feels a wish to kiss her. "Why could he not always love her purely, cleanly?" laments McTeague in his thoughts—or is it the narrator commenting on McTeague?—after he does kiss her (285). Once again, then, we see the "brute" theme, perhaps even more prevalent in Norris than that of the "man's woman," and part of the intersection of subdued sex and open violence in his works.

Norris was usually thought of (certainly during his own lifetime) as violating the standards of gentility then prevalent, because he wrote so much about sexual desire in *Vandover* and *McTeague*. But if those who saw sex as evil had looked past the mere fact that Norris mentioned it, they would have been pleased to see that he was constantly moralizing against it (Dillingham, "Frank Norris and the Genteel Tradition" 17). The first two novels are so daring, in any event, mainly because the author was working on them as a college student, learning to write, and not concerning himself with making a living as a novelist. But in the popular novels—all largely generic and serialized in magazines, as noted—the lust he condemns in his earlier books shrinks into a series of hints and winkings. *Blix* is a story of friendship rather than romance for a good part of the novel—in fact it begins with the couple deciding that they don't love each other. In *Moran*, the hero and heroine are "mates" (Moran often addresses Wilbur by this word) in the nautical sense rather than the romantic-commitment one. And *A Man's Woman*, though Norris's fullest exploration of love, has no sex at all—neither the writer nor, probably, his readers could imagine the bestial Bennett copulating with tall, prim Lloyd.

Even in *The Octopus*, Hilma is not a sex-goddess, despite Norris's impassioned descriptions of her curvy body, just as she is never a mother despite the "crown of motherhood" passages. In fact, she holds onto her innocence better than Trina does in *McTeague*. When Annixter kisses her, she tells him later that she "cried for an hour" to think that he found her so "cheap" (*The Octopus* 741-2). And when he still feels desire for her, thinking even that he can possess her because he is her employer, the Norris who narrated *McTeague* returns, writing of the "lower nature of man ... rous[ing] itself like a hideous and abominable beast" (763). Finally, in *The Pit*, despite its plot of likely adultery, Laura thinks early in the novel that Corthell is the wrong man for her because, with him, relations could only be "sex-relations," and Jadwin appeals to her intellect (31).

So even marriage did not seem to fully convince Frank Norris that sexual desire was not only, as lust alone, a degradation of both man and woman, but a vital part of a fulfilling love-relationship, a symbol as well as realization of a deep bond. He never escaped entirely from the genteel-tradition idea that a woman's role is to influence a man spiritually and morally only—or perhaps, we can speculate, he never escaped from an early guilt at being interested in women not his mother. What remains in the novels, from beginning (girlfriend Turner's attempt to keep Vandover on the straight and narrow way) to end (Laura Jadwin learning from her sister how to support one's warrior-businessman husband), is the image of the "man's woman," Norris's personal fusion of evolutionary theory and Victorian woman-as-Christ doctrine.

"Pres, she's made a man of me," Annixter says to his friend the poet in *The Octopus* (950)—loving her has somehow made him love everybody, and for the rest of his brief time in the novel he is unselfish and caring to such people as Dyke's fatherless family. The "man" he has become has nothing to do with virility, for the blustery, gun-slinging Annixter of *The Octopus*'s first half had no shortage of testosterone. This shows us how far we have progressed since *Moran*, where all Moran has really taught Wilbur, other than some nautical tricks, is how to enjoy violence. In the other middle novels, and the two wheat novels to which they provide a transition, the moral guidance denied to Vandover and McTeague is given by strong, upright, and sometimes semi-masculine women to men who would otherwise blunder childishly (like Condy) or brutally (like Bennett and Annixter) through life.

Pizer feels that Norris's view of the male-female relationship is simplistic, but he is also practically the first critic to have pointed out the middle novels as something other than a trio of lesser works to skip over when considering Norris. If we realize how central the male-female dialectic actually was in the author's life, we can see gender relationships as *more* important than the much-discussed pseudo-naturalist themes in Norris. And gender relationships are exactly what *Moran of the Lady Letty*, *Blix*, and *A Man's Woman* are about.

Critics of the past have been aware of these issues, but for a long time, the critical conversation on Norris, which has now been running on for almost exactly a century, revolved around categories like realism and naturalism more than anything else. Of course some have taken psychoanalytical points of view; most of those who did refer to his family background have noted the pull of his parents' differing characters and wishes for their son. Others have written of the contradictions, the attempts to resolve opposites, in Norris's work, but it is the *connection* between this and his own self-opposing heritage which has not really been made. Mostly, he has been discussed in terms of the familiar literary ideas of his time: first, as he would have preferred—and least accurately—as a naturalist, an heir to Zola; and later with a tangle of 19th-century traditions, such as transcendentalism, romanticism, and the already-discussed Victorian gentility.

Past critical opinion can be divided loosely into three periods: early posthumous reactions which painted him as the American "boy Zola" he wished to be, and considered his early death a loss; 1940s-50s views of Norris from the perspective almost solely of naturalism, judging him by how firmly he followed that method; and 1960s-70s views either recognizing the author's greater debt to other traditions and viewing him positively, or more often, dismissing him according to the old definitions. Since then, Norris, like other American "naturalists," has been viewed by the more discerning critics in completely different ways.

The obituary by Norris patron W.D. Howells in 1902 repeated Howells's influential belief in the younger writer's talent and the major status of *McTeague* and *The Octopus* in particular, calling the first an American *Odyssey* and the second an *Iliad* (775). The famous realist, who had encouraged Norris to publish *McTeague*, had in 1899 written a review in *Literature* describing the novel as "a case in point" to encourage other revolutionary (as he felt Norris was) writers. The book had generally been met on publication by what one critic calls "prudery, priggishness, and Pecksniffery" (Marchand 202) because of its dark and brutal plot (although, as has been observed, it is an example in its own way of the genteel tradition). The struggle for realism may have seemed paramount at the time, but Howells himself, though saying Zola was Norris's literary mentor, saw the "passion for the romantic" in *McTeague* (Howells 773).

During the decade of the teens, Frederic Taber Cooper and Isaac Marcosson published books on various authors including Norris, which presented a boyish literary hero who reflected the clean (a favorite Cooper term) values of his country. Cooper compares Norris repeatedly to Zola, and considers his interest in romanticism his only real fault—a point of view which would come up again among the naturalist critics of the 1950s. Showing that the attitudes of Norris's lifetime had not changed much, Cooper calls *McTeague* repellant, but *Blix* is "a sparkling little love story, clean and wholesome ... free from the embarrassment of sex consciousness" (321). Overall, Norris seemed in 1912 to have "adopted the creed of naturalism ardently, refashioning it to suit the needs of a younger, cleaner civilization, a world of wider expanses, purer air, freer life" (Cooper 297). All of this is perhaps a better reflection on the period of national self-satisfaction in which Norris wrote than on Norris himself; what patriot could not cheer for an author who, in *A Man's Woman*, has Lloyd cry to her conquering husband about the North Pole: "Put that flag there!" (238)?. As difficult as it is to pin down Norris politically—in different books he seems to be socialist, fascist, and all things in between—some distance may have been needed from the Rough Rider era before its most enthusiastic author could be viewed objectively.

The biography by Franklin Walker in 1932 begins this period of greater perceptivity. It has stood for over six decades as the only full-length treatment of Norris's life. To Walker the author was "a boy who barely became a man before he died, but in whom the boyish qualities were the qualities which made him great" (1). Perhaps this is itself a facile view, not so different from Granville Hicks writing soon afterward that "when one remembers his youth, one forgives all his faults" (175), but many valuable facts about the author, revealing more than just his salient characteristic of immaturity, are contained in Walker's book. Without it, the full image of a young man torn between the strong personalities of his parents would not be available.

Paul Bixler's valuable review of Norris's literary reputation in 1934 details the history given above, and the critical near-neglect for many years— Norris was "subordinated to Stephen Crane and Ambrose Bierce," a surprisingly dour and ironic pair to group this essentially naive writer with (120)—until Bixler's own time. Starting with Hicks's mention in 1935's *The Great Tradition,* this neglect began fading and Norris was placed firmly in the ranks of America's naturalists. 1940s critics such as Ernest Marchand (*Frank Norris: A Study*) credited the author with slashing the draperies of romance and chivalry that cloaked American writing in the late 19th century and founding what Marchand called "the red-blooded school in America" (102)—a literary phenomenon linked to Kipling and to Teddy Roosevelt's strenuous life and imperialist conquest. It is true that, as with London, Norris's belief in the Anglo-Saxon's historical inevitability and his pleasure in violent detail point out the author's connection to the decade of the Spanish-American War; but few still seemed able to see his moralistic side.

More than a decade after Marchand, the influential authors Charles Child Walcutt (*American Literary Naturalism, A Divided Stream*) and Lars Ahnebrink (*The Beginnings of Naturalism in American Fiction*) still listed Norris among the naturalists and emphasized his debt to Zola. But it was Walcutt who used the term "natural dynamism"—nature as a conscious, benign force—to correctly describe the philosophy Norris was showing in the wheat books instead of naturalism (146). Though he followed the previous generation of critics in rating Norris lowest when he was least naturalistic, Walcutt was also, by noting the tone of "Sunday-school moral censure" in *Vandover* (124), seeing through a chink of the doorway that was being opened by others to reveal the complete Frank Norris.

Maxwell Geismar is credited by Warren French with having brought Norris back to real critical attention after 1950. Geismar, as noted above, initiated the gender-focused exploration of Norris, in *Rebels and Ancestors,* by hypothesizing a connection between repressed sex and violence. Two years later, Charles Hoffman in the article "Norris and the Responsibility of the Novelist" was pointing out that Norris condemned his ill-fated heroes as a moral judge, rather than as a naturalist; and Kenneth Lynn made his interesting if under-supported argument that Norris was a "mama's boy" whose plots all reflected a passion for his mother and a desire to meet the standards of his Alger-hero father.

Using Walker's biographical details as a foundation (plus a lot of imagination), Lynn argued that Norris disdained his own cultured, dilettantish side—the training as a painter, the interest in literature instilled by his mother and furthered by her support of his writing classes at Harvard—and wished to emulate his father, especially after the divorce and disowning. Though it is argued rather in Lynn's study that the issue is not so much the son wishing to please one parent or the other as feeling throughout his life the pull of what each represented, his service to the critical conversation on Frank Norris was to bring this topic to the forefront for the first time. Sometimes he makes a statement based on nothing but his eagerness to make his point—as when calling this football-cheering fraternity prankster "bookish and shy" (161), or implying that his parents divorced *because* his father was frustrated at being "defeated" in his plans for him (165). But without Lynn's ability to find father-figures and parentally-concerned passages in works as disparate as *The Octopus* and the literary essays—as without Lynn's own clue-provider, Franklin Walker—the theory presented in this book might never have emerged.

The new view that Norris is a romantic moralist and not a naturalist at all—set forth most fully in French's noteworthy *Frank Norris* (1962), which followed a suggestion of Walcutt's in asserting Emerson and transcendentalism as an influence—continued to be expressed in the 1950s. Stanley Cooperman ("Frank Norris and the Werewolf of Guilt") connected the author to Calvinistic determinism, while William B. Dillingham also argued, in "Frank Norris and the Genteel Tradition," that Norris always saw sex as vice. These critics placed the author in the traditions of the century in which he was born, rather than in the amoral, Godless-universe school of his contemporary Crane. Yet it was still possible in that decade for Van Wyck Brooks in *The Confident Years* to again call Norris a "'red-blood' school" founder, and assert that he and London "broke the spell" of the genteel tradition (212, 244). A deeper glimpse into the author appeared in 1962, when George Johnson's article on the frontier and *McTeague*, while focusing on McTeague's escape from the city, revealed much about Norris's conflicts with himself that uncovered the many Yin-Yang pairs that illustrate his entrapment in a dialectic.

During all of these years, the middle novels were ignored, dismissed briefly as well below *McTeague* and *The Octopus* in quality, or in a few cases (like Cooper and Ahnebrink) seen as pleasant or entertaining, but not thematically significant. Even an article focusing on a source for *A Man's Woman* (John C. Sherwood, "Norris and the *Jeannette*") was eager to note that the novel is perhaps Norris's worst book—a familiar but challengeable view. The breakthrough for these novels was in 1964, when Donald Pizer, who may be the best Norris critic, wrote an article on "The Masculine-Feminine Ethic in Frank Norris's Popular Novels" (which became material for his book *The Novels of Frank Norris*), arguing that these "popular" novels are an apprentice trilogy about male-female behavior that precedes the uncompleted wheat trilogy. And fittingly enough, unlike *The Octopus* and its fellow "better" books, endlessly dissected since Norris's death, the three romances are, at least by contrast, as new a frontier as the one closed in Norris's youth had once been.

This new ground is not totally unbroken. The last three decades in Norris criticism show an increase in recognition of the value of these works, and in fact the value of all Norris's work, in spite of—sometimes because of—its author's proud thoughtlessness. When critical opinion could not agree that Norris was not a naturalist, it was unclear what he in fact was, and much of the 1960s' commentary simply focused on condemning his faults. One writer compared him to Cole Porter. Larzer Ziff in *The American 1890s* frequently used the word "impatient" to describe Norris, and argued of the author's claim that style is unimportant: "One cannot have *no* style," just disregard it and thus have bad style (270). Ziff also wrote that Norris's Social Darwinism kept him from being a great writer (257), but Jay Martin in *Harvests of Change* merely noted this Darwinism, and stated an opposite viewpoint to Lynn by writing that Norris felt a compulsion to reject his father (59).

In that decade, some thoughtful writing about the author also raised the debate beyond the sometimes wearying back-and-forth over his strengths and weaknesses seen earlier. In addition to Pizer's perceptivity on many issues in the articles that preceded *The Novels of Frank Norris*, he wrote in *Realism and Naturalism in 19th-Century American Literature* that Norris's rejection of "thought" for "feeling" was an intellectual position itself, which Pizer named "sophisticated primitivism" (107). And Dillingham made the original point in *Frank Norris: Instinct and Art* (1969) that Norris's writings follow his painting attempts along artistic lines, such as subdued color and close observation of detail.

Don Graham and Barbara Hochman, having published entire books on Norris, lead the list of 1970s-80s critics, although they are not the only ones to have made interesting discoveries. Graham, like Hochman, acknowledges the past critical view of Norris as a curiosity or a bad writer, but says (correctly) that he deserves more credit than he's received (3). His theme in *The Fiction of Frank Norris: The Aesthetic Context* is, as one might guess, that the novels are "an inquiry into the nature of aesthetic experience" (16), in which sensitivity is good and sensuousness is bad. Norris's satirization of popular bad taste in *Vandover* (idealization of women in painting) and *Blix* (garishly-decorated indoors v. natural outdoors) is most relevant here, but Graham traces the motif throughout his novels.

Hochman in 1988's *The Art of Frank Norris, Storyteller* finds a theme of the vulnerability of individuals in the world, searching for a control and order which she feels Norris is telling us can be found only in the act of writing itself. (In the process she becomes probably the only critic to compare Norris to John Keats.) Although she also sees something new in the novels, the best modern probing of them comes in articles: Debra Munn revealing a great deal about *Blix* by comparing the magazine serialization to the (revised) published book, Glen A. Love tracing Norris's familiar anti-urban escapism through several novels, and especially, Joseph McElrath's "The Erratic Design of Frank Norris's *Moran of the Lady Letty*". McElrath posits an authorial control and irony that reveal a more sophisticated novel than originally thought—both an effort to please Norris's audience and a parody of the tastes of that very audience.

A few other fresh viewpoints on Norris during the 1980s can be mentioned, particularly on *McTeague:* Walter Benn Michaels's brilliant connection of its gold symbol to 1890s politics in *The Gold Standard and the Logic of Naturalism,* and William Freedman's Freudian article "Oral Passivity and Oral Sadism in Norris's *McTeague.*"

But what we are left with, as always, after the dust of the critics' battles has settled, is the primary work itself.   We can disregard the jejune, Kiplingesque short stories, though a few, like "A Deal in Wheat," cast as clear a light on some themes as the novels do; Norris had little interest in the short story as a genre. Similarly, Norris's journalistic work, especially for the San Francisco *Wave,* is little different from that of other competent young hacks of the day, and worth reading now only by those interested in the author's apprenticeship. What remains is the uneven but mostly sincere and forceful literary creed laid out in the essay collection *The Responsibilities of the Novelist,* and seven novels whose characters re-enact the struggle between roughness and refinement, spirit and nature—the elemental woman and man, Yin and Yang.

The life of the man who wrote these novels is, in large part, a story about the same struggle.

2

Frank Norris and His Time

WHEN Gertrude Doggett, a Puritan-stock maiden from a small New England village, quit the stage to marry Benjamin Franklin Norris, Sr., the frontier was still open and one of America's key moments of definition, the Civil War, had only recently ended. The story of this union of a willful, talented woman and a businessman who promised—perhaps meaning it at the time, perhaps not— not to curb her career or her independent character can be read in detail in *The Pit*, for three decades later, as noted, this couple's eldest son would fictionalize his parents as Curtis and Laura Jadwin.

Laura has been called one of Norris's most fully-realized female characters more than once. Rather than merely condemning her selfishness as many critics do (and many readers must be tempted to do), Warren French shows insight into this novel which he, almost alone, admires by describing the struggle which creates this self-absorbed character. Laura faces up to, and finally escapes, the social pressures of the stifling Massachusetts town of her upbringing, perhaps as conformist a place as any "Main Street" imagined by Sinclair Lewis. When the town sends a group of "lady-deaconesses" to tell her to behave properly and not think of being an actress, she throws them out violently, and leaves for Chicago later that month (*The Pit* 40-1). There is a price to her spirit, though: "The stubborn pride that makes the gesture possible lingers on after the revolt has succeeded, in the form of an excessive love of self and suspicion of others." She becomes afraid of marriage because she might "lose the individuality that she has purchased at the price of exile from her home" (French 110).

Walker's biography does not delve into the character of Frank, Jr.'s mother before her marriage, but the parallels in *The Pit* are so great that the reader suspects Norris himself to be an accurate biographer. (Don Graham maintains that Frank's brother Charles asserted that the Jadwins did represent their parents.) (127) When Laura first tells her friend Mrs. Cressler that she will marry Jadwin, her reasons seem empty, amounting to little more than a surrender to force. "Do you suppose you can say 'no' to that man." (Mrs. Cressler's response: "I might have known he'd have you if he set out to do it.") Love?—"Yes, I think I love him very much—sometimes. And then sometimes I think I don't. I can't tell" (*The Pit* 151, 153). What reasons the future Mrs. Norris did have for choosing her husband we don't know—but if Norris is thinking of his parents in this scene as well, he seems significantly unable (or unwilling) to recall a strong, romantic bond behind their union. And Frank Norris, Sr., like the fictional Jadwin, would in fact be more successful as a businessman than as a caring husband.

Frank was born and raised in Chicago, where his father had a successful wholesale jewelry house. Though the elder Norris *was* a self-made man, Frank turned his history, via Jadwin, into the standard American-dream tale—Algerism once again. Mrs. Cressler tells Laura, when "selling" Jadwin as a future husband, "His people were farmers, nothing more nor less than hardy, honest fellows," and he had little schooling and no money at first (*The Pit* 69). Images of this humble rural beginning, viewed rather mistily by the urban-born Norris, appear in Jadwin's own recollections throughout the novel; readers can at least be relieved that he was not born in an actual log cabin.

Jadwin's fortune, like Vandover's father's, is made through real estate. Norris's father had a different profession, but the parallels continue: the home where his brothers Charles (also to be a novelist) and Lester were born and where he himself lived until the age of eleven was the model for the Jadwins' house in the novel—a grand mansion with stables, coachman, and all (Walker 13-4). We also learn from Walker the Jadwin-like detail of the elder Norris's admiration for Dwight Moody's "notion that business principles were as good in religion as they were on La Salle Street" (14). Curtis Jadwin and Frank Norris, Sr. both passed on this 19th-century canard to the younger generation by teaching a Sunday-school class. One hopes that there was more subtlety to the views of the author's father than are shown in this motto which Norris put into the mouth of Jadwin: "not slothful in business, fervent in spirit, praising the Lord" (*The Pit* 117).

Meanwhile, Frank's mother was instilling literature into her sons, and perhaps exercising the stage skills she had lost in marriage along with her career, by reading Scott and Dickens aloud to them. However well-known Norris's self-endowed title of the "boy Zola" may be, it is these British authors, rather than the French naturalists, whose influence can be seen most in his novels. Scott's large, romantic canvas is imitated in *The Octopus* and elsewhere, while characters from the endlessly magazine-binding Grannis and the endlessly tea-drinking Miss Baker in *McTeague*, to Annixter in *The Octopus* (who is himself reading *David Copperfield* when the story begins) are Dickensian in their one or two exaggerated, often-repeated actions or spoken phrases. Fittingly enough, Laura Jadwin reads aloud regularly to her husband—they have no children—although his tastes are a bit lower, and he especially likes Stevenson's *The Wrecker*, a sea yarn much like *Moran* (and, many think, an influence on both that novel and *McTeague*).

Although Norris's initial artistic attempts were in painting (as were the autobiographical Vandover's), it is tempting to think that he turned finally to writing with this early maternal influence planted firmly in his psyche. Some facts support this assumption: Gertrude Norris paid $400 toward the publication of her son's first book, the Scott-like poetic ballad *Yvernelle* (Pizer, notes to *Frank Norris: Novels and Essays*), and she also sent Frank to Harvard to study writing for a year which commenced just as his parents divorced. Did this split mean that the mother could finally have her own plans for her son realized, with the powerful father and his take-over-the-business plans gone? Certainly Lynn believes this; "of course," he writes, Gertrude moved to Cambridge herself during the Harvard year to keep a maternal eye on her son. "The man who had tricked her out of the life she should have had would never again be allowed to tamper with her son's career. Quite definitely, Junior was going to be a writer, not a businessman" (Lynn 165).

But though the simplicity of this view is tempting, Frank seemed happiest at first with the many masculine influences on his youthful life, and what Lynn sees as his feminine side is, in part, simply his early inability to keep with discipline to his own plans. After the family's move to California in 1883, Frank was sent away to school, where he broke his arm playing football. To Lynn, this was an ignominious experience, and a central event in forming the boy's despair at not being "manly" enough to please his father (166). To Walker, it was simply a chance for Frank to relax and recuperate at home in San Francisco, watching cowboys, parades, and "best of all," military activities from his window (21). Certainly the adult Norris never forgot this failure; he has Vandover try without success to join football at Harvard (*Vandover and the Brute* 13). But what is most significant is that it was the first of a string of failures.

Walker himself judges that Frank Norris, Sr.'s business ambitions for his son conflicted with his wife's artistic ones, but the man was not really inflexible in this conflict. Frank's father agreed to send him to the San Francisco Art Association, but the boy—to whom, as to Vandover, the most threatening deadly sin was probably sloth rather than lust—disliked the exercises and constant drilling in the studio. "He wanted to do things on a grand scale," and spent his days sketching horses instead (Walker 25). At the same time, he was beginning the lead-soldier games with Charles mentioned in his dedication to his younger brother in *The Pit*. The "Gaston le Fox" stories Frank wrote, based on these imaginary wars, must have been his first literary efforts.

When Frank was 17, his younger brother Lester died. How was this event significant to the parents and the other children? We don't know; Walker barely mentions Lester, and the sort of critical fodder one might hope for (as when O'Neill fictionalized his dead baby brother with his *own* first name, Eugene, in *Long Day's Journey Into Night*) do not appear in Norris's writing. Thus we can only speculate, particularly on how much more protective of and concerned with correctly molding her remaining sons Gertrude Norris might have been.

In any event, the Norris family left the scene of their sorrows behind and went to Paris the year Lester died, but all of the most tempting critical connections one could draw from this visit refuse to fully materialize. Frank learned French, but there is no evidence that he discovered Zola and his fellow naturalists at this time. He attended the Atelier Julien, but was more impressed by the chivalric images and operatic pageantry of Paris than attentive, as a man who shared his mother's artistic soul might be, to the demands of learning to paint (Walker 27). Left alone after his parents' and brother's departure, he made notes of the armor in the Invalides for a planned big battle picture, and his first published work (*San Francisco Chronicle*, March 31, 1889) was about armor. During this year, Frank Norris's interest gradually turned from art to writing.

Again, it is not virility but discipline that the elder Norris found lacking in his son. When the businessman discovered the episodes of "Robert D'Artois," an apparent continuation of the old lead-soldier epic, that Norris was sending home to Charles, his father demanded that he return. Just as it was his son's failure to return to the football field, rather than some weakness in having gotten hurt, that must have irked this priest of "business principles," it was his refusal to finally take painting seriously that made his father put an end to the Paris interlude. Vandover, too, had planned a grand-scale painting on a bloody topic—"The Last Enemy," a picture of a lion stalking a wounded man—which never actually appeared on canvas; and as Donald Pizer has pointed out, many of Norris's basic worries about his own character were dramatized in Vandover's (*The Novels of Frank Norris* 33). Paris, like his football attempt, remained in Norris's mind; in addition to his dramatizing the surprisingly boisterous life of the Atelier Julien in the story "This Animal of a Buldy Jones," he has Corthell retreat to Paris both times he is rejected by Laura Jadwin, and the city hovers over *Vandover and the Brute* as a never-realized goal for Vandover.

Back home, the now-adult Norris continued to face the art v. commerce struggle which would become part of the dialectic in his work. Still determined to see him inherit his jewelry concern, his father sent him to the University of California at Berkeley, which he attended for four years without (due to a repeatedly-failed math exam) ever getting a degree. Walker says that the young man was still mostly playing at this time, including at the hazing and pranks of fraternity mock-warfare (49)—and at writing. It was at this point that, with maternal support, *Yvernelle* was published. In fact, Gertrude herself had also submitted the armor article, so that both Norris's first published works are preserved only through his mother's efforts.

At this point the struggle must have been clearly delineated to all three parties concerned. One can imagine the businessman's feelings as his wife, who may already have become his adversary in other ways as the marriage-bond began to break, pressed her role as the "doting mother" determined to see her son's artistic, not business, talent nurtured. Whether Frank, Jr. *had* any business talent is debatable, but this probable deficiency certainly did not go unnoticed by the son himself. Not only do powerful capitalists appear as heroes in his writing, but he more subtly tries in his literary essays to portray *himself*, though a novelist, as a member of the great American world of commerce.

One more issue is worth noting as we pass beyond Norris's youth and origins: his view of the less-privileged masses, or what he often capitalizes in his writing as "the People." Was this rich man's child classist as well as racist? It is interesting that Presley, who many believe is based on Norris, feels that "uncouth brutes of farmhands and petty ranchers, grimed with the soil they worked upon, were odious to him beyond words. Never could he feel in sympathy with them" (*The Octopus* 581). Yet the ranchers, as well as the farm workers, are often called "the People," the mob, in *The Octopus*. And the simple fact is, they are not; they are rich men like Norris's father, large landowners. Perhaps this is why Norris is inconsistent in his literary essays, calling the People "the real seekers after Truth," who "pronounce final judgment" on literature through their popular opinion, in "The Responsibilities of the Novelist" (*Frank Norris: Novels and Essays* 1208), yet writing elsewhere that they are being fooled by the "lies" of merely venal writers. In his novels, this child of privilege sometimes laughed at the lower classes; but it seems that, ultimately, he could not decide who the People really are.

College students in his day, of course, were hardly likely to be from poor backgrounds, and Frank Norris is a perfect example of one who could attend a university only because his parents bought him a place. And this semi-painter, semi-writer, who would later reject intellectualism out of his guilt at failing academically, lost his last chance to please his father by his actions at Berkeley.

Warren French asserts that Norris never did anything that did not come naturally, including at college; this seems too harsh a view, as novel-writing (as well as all the research Norris did for *The Octopus* and *The Pit*) does require much discipline. But it is a partial description of his Berkeley days, when fraternity hell-raising—"The fraternity reassures man of his natural goodness," French notes (20)—took up more of his energy than learning to do sums. Norris's wistful view of this "reassuring" period of camraderie (like that of an army?) colors several of his novels: Presley and Annixter attended unnamed Eastern colleges, and Vandover is a Harvard clone with standard details of campus dress and behavior. Most absurd, though, is the motif of Ross Wilbur's Yale background, which helps him become a successful seaman and fighter, in *Moran*.

But Norris did do more during his four years than haze frat pledges— he took writing classes, for he had apparently almost decided now (with his mother's firm hand guiding him) to be a writer. Years later Norris wrote angrily of the formulaic demands of writing teachers at Berkeley, rebellion against whom probably contributed to his scorn for "style." One professorial comment on Norris, quoted by Walker, is worth noting, however, because it almost sums up the author's writing: "Student essays are seldom very good or very bad, but about twelve years ago I received one that was both" (54-5).

Also at Berkeley, Norris learned evolution from Le Conte, and became what Walker calls a "regular fellow"—cheering football players rather than Scott-novel knights, and revelling in the masculine atmosphere of the only lengthy period in his first 25-odd years during which his mother was not present. Like Vandover, he frequented saloons and played poker, and he had also now discovered Zola, possibly in the French classes which he took, characteristically enough, because he already spoke French. More interested in the Continental novelist's status as a shocker of Americans than in the details of his theory, Norris was (in one of Walker's most-quoted passages) "frequently seen about the campus with a French paper edition of Zola under his arm and was always ready to stop and defend the novelist" (82).

Meanwhile, his parents' marriage was crumbling. Frank Norris, Sr. went on a world trip in 1892 without his family, and in 1894, he and Gertrude divorced. As noted, only Frank, Jr. was excluded from the settlement, a scathing symbol of the businessman's final disappointment. Walker, like others, believes that the son was now free to write and thus to get what was certainly valuable guidance at Harvard from Lewis Gates—but did he really feel free? *Vandover*, written shortly afterward, was partly an imitation of Zola's character-in-decay novels, but was mainly an emotional blend of guilt, apologies and fear. Anyone who reads this novel—whose hero longs for his dead mother and despises himself for disappointing his imperious father, the "Governor"—with any knowledge of Norris's life can feel the double-bind churning painfully through the author's innards. Everything that happens to Vandover, particularly the deaths of both his parents, he feels personally responsible for, just as Norris might well have felt for the end of the marriage. Reading the closing pages of the novel, or the passage where the narrator degrades his character by describing him lying in vomit with flies buzzing around, one can imagine young Norris furiously writing these words and fearing—or wishing—similar punishment to fall on himself.

William Dillingham describes a young man, Norris at the point of his departure from Berkeley, who could be either Norris or Vandover: a man "who hates laziness but is plagued by it, who admires strength and activity but is far from robust, who is extremely ambitious and single-minded in purpose but is unsure of himself" (*Frank Norris: Instinct and Art* 29). Except for the words "single-minded in purpose," which he probably was not, this passage perfectly captures the conflicts still raging in the 24-year-old Norris. It is easy to believe Lynn's argument that, though the father ignored the son for the rest of his life, Norris always wanted to succeed in his eyes.

And so, after Harvard, came his attempts to join in that most manly of activities, war. He did indeed see the raw and terrible "life" that he found better than "literature" in both South Africa and Cuba, but his exits from both countries were as unheroic as his exam-failing departure from Berkeley. Instead of fighting for Anglo-Saxons against the "sluggish" and "stupid"

Boers, he caught a serious fever and was finally given 24 hours from the government to get out of the country (Walker 110). And his experience of the Spanish-American War two years later consisted of waiting in Florida with many other would-be correspondents (including Crane), and then in the summer, having a real jungle adventure, seeing battles and starving people, and getting fever again. Significantly, though he was seeking virility in these endeavors, it was the feminine representative of his Yin-Yang battle who finally captured him once again, when his mother cared for him during both of his periods of recuperation (Hart, introduction to *A Novelist in the Making* 28, 31).

Between these direct forays into the violence he otherwise only wrote about, Norris continued to write. His apprenticeship at the San Francisco *Wave* is essentially described in *Blix*—what is most interesting about this period is that the magazine backed Collis Huntington, head of the Southern Pacific Railroad, a man and an institution who would become the ultimate male-power figure, Shelgrim, and his "Pacific and Southwestern Railroad" in *The Octopus*. Norris also finished his first two novels, *Vandover* and *McTeague*, which had germinated and flowered mainly at Harvard. His surviving Harvard themes, which are collected in *A Novelist in the Making*, provide a glimpse into the creation of these novels, as well as of *Blix*, with which they were intertwined at this early stage. *Moran of the Lady Letty*, the first middle novel (sometimes mistakenly called Norris's first novel, since it was published before the collegiate works), was serialized in the *Wave*.

It was natural for the adult Norris to first make San Francisco his home, though he also worked for *McClure's Magazine* in New York in 1897, a phase which helped establish his career, and spent his last year, while working on *The Pit*, in New York as well. Ironically, though Norris gladly accepted Eastern jobs for the money (especially when he married) and perhaps prestige, he had Presley, after his success with the poem "The Toilers," reject the "cheap reward" of a career there. Instead, "the struggle [in California] had its poet" (*The Octopus* 890).

And San Francisco, at first, had its novelist. In his youth, Walker writes, the city "capture[d] his heart" and "became his home at a time when he was beginning to look for romance in his surroundings, whereas Chicago had been for him a matter of dreary weather and dancing schools" (16-7). This aura of romance, though subdued in *McTeague* (where the wilderness is the brutish hero's true home), bursts forth in *Blix* with its evocation of all the city's aspects—Chinatown, the harbor with its ships, etc.—as seemingly existing purely for the pleasure of young lovers. And James Hart has pointed out that San Francisco made more subtle appearances in Norris's novels—a few of *Vandover*'s characters (Haight, Geary) are named after streets in the city (introduction to *A Novelist in the Making* 3).

Norris tried to make this personal response to his adolescent home seem like a literary position when he wrote in an 1897 essay that San Francisco is a perfect setting for fiction. "But who shall be our"—i.e., the American West's—"Kipling? Where is the man ... that shall go a-gunning for stories up and down our streets and into our houses and parlors" ("An Opening for Novelists," *Frank Norris: Novels and Essays* 1113) Obviously, he wanted the thunderous public response to this question to be: "Benjamin Franklin Norris!"

Which side of the dialectic does this city belong on—is it "mother" or "father" territory? In one sense it seems to be completely the second; not only is the effete and womanish East scorned by Norris in such writings as the story "Dying Fires," in which Overbeck's wonderfully coarse and Western writer's muse is wrecked by the New York literary set, but New England was Gertrude Norris's firm background. Again, the character of the author's mother may be best represented by his own creation Laura Jadwin. Chapter Two of *The Pit* starts by telling of her hometown of Barrington, Mass., where her passion for literature and acting was stifled by the "'New England spirit' ... a sort of religion, wherein the Old Maid was the priestess, the Spinster the officiating devotee, the thing worshipped the Great Unbeautiful, and the ritual unremitting, unrelenting Housework" (40). Despite this almost feminist protest which her son wrote down (perhaps remembering things she herself had said), Gertrude probably regarded the older culture of her upbringing above that of California. Thus she encouraged Harvard as her son's choice of a writing school, and lived with Charles in Cambridge while Frank was there.

Yet, as the above passage on Laura suggests, there was a sense of emancipation in California for Gertrude as well as for her oldest son. Ahnebrink wrote that the West's women, like its men, had to be strong and courageous, and that (though his source for this information is unknown) Norris's mother herself was something of a "new woman" (18). The relevance of this to Norris's female characters will be discussed later. The point here is that California represents *both* masculine and feminine to Norris. Not only does the "art" of emasculated men like Hartrath arrive in San Francisco via Mrs. Cedarquist's women's club in *The Octopus* ("The Renaissance had appeared in the West," says the narrator with heavy irony) (827), but the state's rural (in *The Octopus*) and wild (in *McTeague*) areas, plus the ocean that borders it (in *Moran* and somewhat in *Blix*) all appear as womb-like, Great Mother symbols. Perhaps this is why Norris oddly calls the Eastern-bred Laura "a daughter of the frontier" at one point (*The Pit* 60)—the two battling halves blended somehow in his mother's presence in California, and thus left the state, and the city of San Francisco, as a place of central importance in both his life and his work.

During his time with the *Wave*, Norris had a period of writer's block—Walker feels that he was upset at the apparent impossibility of publishing the frank-themed *Vandover* and *McTeague*, and did not want to be a hack writer all his days (144). Lynn, as in describing his football attempt, is more eager to see Norris as a psychological case, calling the writing break "some sort of nervous collapse" (180). But it should be noted that, while suffering from guilt and perhaps from uncertainty about sex. Norris was not abnormal, though this prolonged analysis may create such an impression. His personal conflicts are interesting chiefly because they reflect the conflicts of frontier-closing America, when men (and perhaps women) could not decide whether the rough, expansive power of the past was still appropriate.

A personal dilemma, if not a national one, can sometimes be eased by the entrance of one good person; and as noted, Jeannette Black appeared at just this crucial point. Not only did the romance with her free Norris somewhat from his maternal dependence, but it helped clarify for him the dilemma of "civilized" shelter v. passion and romance. In the middle novels the polite society of California, the "set" which Norris's mother tried to keep him within, is condemned repeatedly. Much of *Moran*'s first chapter, in which Ross Wilbur's pre-Moran life of debutantes and cotillions is seen, is one loud laugh at this world; and in *Blix*, after noting that Condy and Travis/Blix "went out" (his own quotes) in the San Francisco "Younger Set," Norris describes thoughts of Condy's that were almost certainly his own, too. "He had had experience—all the experience he wanted—with other older women and girls of society. They were sophisticated, they were all a little tired, they had run the gamut of amusements—in a word, they were jaded" (120). Travis, only nineteen like Jeannette, is "unspoiled" by attention to such conventional rules as tolerating one upper-class man, Jack Carter, who gets drunk and tries to force himself on women. Later Carter vengefully says of her that "somehow the best people have dropped her" (241)—but in reality Norris must have felt that he had found the best person for *himself* in this fresh, young, and yet mature girl.

In addition to these other benefits, the romance may have ended his writer's block. After the events described in *Blix*, ending with Jeannette leaving California for school (as does Blix), Norris took leave from his job and went to the Big Dipper mine, which both inspired and gave him peace to write the ending of *McTeague*. Then came *Moran of the Lady Letty*, the Spanish-American War episode, and *A Man's Woman*, written during a convalescent winter in New York—which is why, in Walker's view, the novel has such a gruesome and "pervading air of the sick-room" (215). *McTeague* and *Blix* were published in 1899, and *A Man's Woman* in 1900.

Then came the epic of wheat. *McClure's* let Norris go back to California on salary to research *The Octopus*, where he learned about events which inspired some of those in the novel (the fatal Mussel Slough battle between ranchers and a marshal's deputies, and two men who robbed trains, like the fictional Dyke, after being harmed by the railroad). Staying at the Santa Anita ranch, a writer and effectively an outsider observing details of rural California life, Norris was strikingly similar to Presley in the novel. He even talked to Huntington during its composition, as Presley does to Shelgrim. For *The Pit*, he moved to Chicago (returning to his birthplace just before, although he didn't know it, his death), again gathering masses of facts to provide novelistic detail like a good disciple of Zola.

Norris was not alone in Chicago. In January 1900 (fittingly enough, at the beginning of the new century) he married Jeannette. His new job was as a reader for Doubleday, where, as many have noted, he was instrumental in securing the publication of Dreiser's *Sister Carrie*, the debut of a novelist who was until recently also limited to the "American-naturalist" tag. This job, plus Norris's royalties, had made the marriage consummation financially possible. The couple had a daughter, also named Jeannette, in 1902, the year *The Pit* was completed. The foreword by Juliet Wilbur Tompkins to Volume 9 (*The Pit*) of Norris's collected works gives a brief image of the couple's married life. Norris would say, "Je suis bon bourgeois, moi," and "made a rite of dressing for dinner" with his wife (viii). Perhaps his dilettantish side which Paris had helped instill was returning now that he felt secure. (Perhaps, also—despite the belief of a few critics that the writer of *The Octopus* was a socialist—he was pleased to observe that he had become "bourgeois" like his father, but without his father's help.) There is also a description of Norris's pleasure in being "master in his own house" and commanding his wife (ix) which reminds us of Ross Wilbur's mastering of Moran.

It was the final and probably happiest period in the author's life. Norris was full of plans at this point, for a trip around the world to research *The Wolf*, the intended third volume of the trilogy (Walker believes he never wrote a word of it, but Isaac Marcosson's book says that Norris had all the notes and early chapters done, and his brother Charles would write the novel), for another trilogy about the battle of Gettysburg, and to buy a ranch south of San Francisco.

But a final twist was to end the story of Frank Norris. After enjoying less than a year as both husband and father, and perhaps finally feeling, as head of his own family rather than the inheritor of battling parental wishes, some freedom from his dialectic, Norris himself—not his mother or father—became the ultimate loser of the battle. In October 1902, this man whose health was very weak, primarily because of his efforts to be manly in South Africa and Cuba, manfully ignored an attack of indigestion. But it was a perforated appendix, and the attack led to peritonitis and death. His efforts to be worthy of his now-dead father had indirectly claimed his life as well.

The Political Norris

Seventeen years after Norris's death, his admirer Marcosson wrote of his character: "He was strong and gentle and brave. His aim was lofty and his inspiration boundless. His death was a definite and serious blow to literature" (241). Exaggerated this may be, but again, there was reason for patriots of the era—especially at this later point when America had entered the world stage as participant, and shared victor, in the Great War—to look upon this prophet of Anglo-Saxon conquest so favorably. Norris was not primarily a political author; he believed that plot rather than ideology was the driving factor in a novel, even though the focus on railroad monopolies in *The Octopus* and over-powerful futures traders in *The Pit* led some to rank him with Upton Sinclair as a turn-of-the-century muckraker. But the political background of his time, as noted, helps to illuminate the battles between countries and peoples (and perhaps between men and women) in the novels.

Almost nothing happens in *Blix* that suggests a world outside the two lovers and their "set." But *Moran* contains one of the most striking, and insistently repetitive, examples of Norris's racial attitudes: the dull-witted, simian Chinese that Moran and Wilbur fight. The Spanish-American War also becomes a plot element when Wilbur finally plans to go "filibustering" to Cuba. And in *A Man's Woman*, the focus is on man against nature (or rather against Jung's "Terrible Mother" archetype, as we will see later) until the end of the novel, when an English attempt to reach the Pole helps to force Bennett out of retirement—since, as Lloyd says, "we—America—ought to do it ... Why shouldn't *our* flag be first at the Pole? We who have had so many heroes, such great sailors, such splendid leaders, such explorers" (209, 211). The remaining pages of the novel are soaked in this nationalistic brine, the intriguing love story which dominated earlier having almost totally vanished.

The issue of politics is relevant to Norris's struggle with opposing sides as well. Johnson's point that the author's era could not resolve dilemmas itself recalls what Richard Chase wrote about democracy and American fiction. Unlike European novels which try to "civilize" dilemmas, the American romance is based on contradictions, "the profound poetry of disorder." Democracy itself is not like the shared, inherited institutions of the Old World—it is an either-or choice (14). Norris was hardly unfamiliar with such choices. The unity which he sought at the end of *The Octopus* would be, in this view, at odds with the culture about which the novel is written.

Overall, Norris's politics, as noted, are hard to classify. But we can find a few definite themes in his writing that are consistent; one is exaltation of the American businessman. This is seen not only in previously-mentioned characters such as Cedarquist and Jadwin, but in those same closing pages of *A Man's Woman*, when a trio of cameo-role Cedarquists come to Bennett's house to persuade him to make another effort at the Pole. Norris makes the symbolism of their differing professions all too obvious—"three great and highly-developed phases of 19th-century intelligence—science, manufactures, and journalism" (229)—and it is the manufacturer, the author's greatest hero, who makes the proposal in the person of a past suitor of Lloyd's named Campbell. "I'm afraid we are men more of action than of art, literature, and the like," says Campbell in a long speech, thus echoing Norris's familiar dialectic, and then promises to back an all-American quest for the Pole (232). The word "American" appears thirteen times in the paragraph in which he proposes this. This is the scene ending in Lloyd jamming an American flag's pole into the North Pole on a map and crying, "Put that flag there!"

Another political theme, just as conventional as the one above, appears in this scene: a populist distrust of elected officials. Congress, says Campbell, backed out of raising the money for this great American quest. So who supports it when it begins?—spiritually, that is, since Lloyd actually puts up the money from her fortune—once again, of course, it's "the People, the crowd," seeing Bennett's ship ("the hope of an entire nation") off from the city harbor (241). That same tattered American flag, rescued from the explorer's first disastrous mission, is, effectively enough, now crowning his ship. And a battleship fires a salute, reminding us of the author's third most frequent political theme, the support of wars and conquest already noted.

The background to Norris as a political writer contains many of the points already discussed: his lifetime that combined the 19th and 20th centuries as well as East and West; his pursuit of wars and admiration of armies or of their symbol, football players; and most notably his painful relationship with his father. This latter issue is what probably most influenced his initial individualistic conservatism. Businessmen *were* heroes to Norris, as his comparing them to the Christian warrior Richard the Lionhearted suggests—and this comparison also reminds us that Norris began as a writer about medieval armor, and of medieval balladry (*Yvernelle*). The jeweler's son always had the image shining before him of a strong, even ruthless, but moral and admirable man, the kind of man whose admiration he wanted to gain. (*Being* such a man must have seemed impossible to him after his early failures.) And so the idea of the hero, an idea also appearing in the Norse sagas and American Westerns he enjoyed, stands behind many of Norris's male characters.

This is Curtis Jadwin as Laura first sees him: "a merchant prince, a great financial captain ... Those broad, strong hands, and keen, calm eyes would enfold and envelop a Purpose with tremendous strength, and they would persist and persist and persist, unswerving, unwavering, untiring, till the Purpose was driven home" (*The Pit* 18, 30). The latter sentence shows us two of Norris's most familiar style-markers, hammering overstatement and use of a capital-lettered theme. What is Jadwin's "Purpose" and the purpose of capitalists like him? (The word "capitalist" was certainly not pejorative to Norris; he used it for Jadwin in this same first chapter, and his father even listed his profession as "capitalist" in the city directory.) Walker feels that Norris could not see something so simple and materialistic as actual money-making as his businessman-hero's goal. Jadwin's character, the biographer writes, is meant to show "that the business baron was motivated by the excitement of making a fortune rather than by the desire for money," though his portrayal as a gambler (Norris's general symbol for vice) suggests some ambivalence (293).

It is true that Jadwin is a character whom Norris views with uncertainty, sometimes exalting him and sometimes showing him demeaned by his speculating passion. This is not surprising, since he is based on the author's father. Simpler portrayals of Gilded Age heroes occur in *The Octopus*: the larger-than-life Shelgrim and Cedarquist, whom Glen A. Love rightly calls the real hero of the novel (18). Although Annixter's transformation through love and Vanamee's mystical regeneration story are important in the novel, and thus would arguably make these men its heroes, their themes are most relevant to the late (post-Jeannette) Norris. The pronouncements of the San Francisco manufacturer and shipping magnate Cedarquist are ideas which the writer put forth throughout his career.

"We don't want public statues, and fountains, and park extensions, and gingerbread fetes. We want business enterprise," Cedarquist says to Presley when we first meet him (*The Octopus* 817)—and again we hear Norris behind him, calling out his endlessly-repeated sentence, "We don't want literature, we want life!" Yet Cedarquist admires Presley (whom he is related to, appropriately, through his wife) and speaks with encouragement of his "very great Poem." Here again, as in the end of this novel and in the significance of California generally, we can see the author striving to unite his opposing sides. Cedarquist respects literature, or art, which *is* "life," but rejects that represented by the absurd Hartrath, his wife's protege. In this couple the maternal side of Norris's dialectic is represented negatively by Mrs. Cedarquist, an ignorant "fashionable woman" who wastes money supporting artistic and religious fakes (824). She is what Laura might have become if she had used her energy on women's clubs rather than on pursuit of her husband's love—a burlesque, like the character called "K.D.B." in *Blix*, of Gertrude Norris.

And the positive maternal image, *combined* (thus fulfilling Norris's greatest wish) with the male hero described above, is represented in Cedarquist. He is more moral than Jadwin, saying that the trusts and corruption depicted in the novel are allowed by "the one crying evil of American life," the "indifference" of the again-capitalized People (818). And he repeats the author's own theme in the essay "The Frontier Gone at Last" by saying that Anglo-Saxon imperialism should now go westward (to the East) with markets, not war. As he sees Presley off on his trip to India at the novel's end, he says, "Tell the men of the East to look out for the men of the West. The irrepressible Yank is knocking at the doors of their temples and he will want to sell 'em carpet-sweepers for their harems and electric light plants for their temple shrines" (1095). Shrewd businessman though he is, he also, like Vandover's father at first, accepts the novel's Norris-based character (in this case, Presley) as an artist.

In the same novel we find Norris's most controversial figure, Shelgrim. He is certainly based on Collis Huntington, whom the San Francisco *Wave* had backed—Pizer sees the physical description of Shelgrim in *The Octopus* as corresponding to Huntington, "moth spots" and all (Notes to *Frank Norris: Novels and Essays*). But his famous speech on "force" makes him Norris's masculine principle incarnate. Critics have argued, ever since Hicks's early comment that Norris admired both Huntington and Shelgrim and "could see no flaw" in the character's argument (172), over whether the author shared Presley's semi-convinced bewilderment after hearing the speech, or condemned it. Probably, as befits a man torn by conflict, he did both. Ernest Marchand is correct in telling us that Shelgrim's excuses are unconvincing; there are not simply two alternatives of cruel, corrupt business practice v. bankruptcy (156). But he (and other readers) can see this simply because he is not Frank Norris. The first description of Shelgrim in the novel, long before we meet him, extols him as "a giant figure in the end-of-the-century finance ... symbolic of ungovernable forces ... colossal intellect operating the width of an entire continent" (659). In short, he is the largest of Norris's father-figures— and probably a father-figure to the bemused Presley as well—not a real individual whose arguments Norris can logically examine, but another attempt to transcend the Yin-Yang split through sheer size.

Such characters show that Norris was not really a socialist in *The Octopus*. Lynn observes that he even makes the novel's ranchers richer than the real-life victims of Mussel Slough (187), thus lessening any class-warfare theme the story might have produced. And as for his condemnation of the railroad, this was as conventional a political stand in the 1890s as cheering on American polar explorers. "[A]ttacking a trust at that time," Pizer points out in *The Novels of Frank Norris*, "represented little more social involvement than attacking Communism today" (120). In any event, Norris would have himself argued against political conclusions being drawn from the novel. In the essay "The Novel with a 'Purpose,'" he tells us that the story is the main thing in any novel, not pamphleteering. "Do you think that Mrs. Stowe was more interested in the slave question than she was in the writing of *Uncle Tom's Cabin?*" (*Frank Norris: Novels and Essays* 1198) His understanding of Harriet Beecher Stowe seems flawed, but this is some evidence that, as Pizer and others have said, he was interested in the drama inherent in the Mussel Slough massacre, not the conclusions that could be drawn from the event.

And yet, immediately after remarking that a writer cares about his characters, not the real-life catastrophes that often inspire their existence, Norris contradicts himself with one of the best passages in his literary essays, answering those who claim they see enough suffering in real life to want to read it in fiction. "Do they? Is this really true? The people who buy novels are the well-to-do people. They belong to a class whose whole scheme of life is concerned solely with an aim to avoid the unpleasant ... If there is much pain in life, all the more reason that it should appear in a class of literature which, in its highest form, is a sincere transcription of life" (*Frank Norris: Novels and Essays* 1199). Those who feel that the writer became more compassionate and liberal after his father disowned him may well have a point.

What was consistent, whether he was conservative or liberal, was

Norris's adherence to a standard American belief—romantic individualism. Pizer defines this as "faith in the validity of the individual experience and mind as a source of knowledge and a guide to action," one of the chief reasons American "naturalists" were largely more optimistic than their French forebears ("Romantic Individualism in Garland, Norris and Crane" 468). Thus Norris was unable to regard characters as impersonal "cases," though Zola's theory inclined to this view.   He would not, however, let belief in the individual become an excuse for what Horton and Edwards in their book named "Political Darwinism," and a character like Geary in *Vandover*, with his constant rationalizing of selfishness, shows this.

It is easy to mistake such quasi-moral populism for a simple right-wing attitude. A view of Norris from the other side of the old Iron Curtain, written by a pre-revolution Czech critic, shows how an American from the Teddy Roosevelt era appears to one trained to think in Communist terms.

Thus Vladimir Smrz of Prague's Charles University wrote that the "bourgeoisie" Norris represented "the conservative Right-Center" of his time which believed that unions were dangerous and worshipped businessmen. Echoing Walker, Smrz cited the writer's view of economic conflict as "an amoral romance of heroic adventure ... the great financier is motivated in his ventures not by the love of money, but, like the warrior, by his love of the excitement of battle" (19, 32). This approach becomes laborious when Smrz tries so hard to use *The Octopus* to show that capitalism is evil that he praises its sentimental and cliched parts as most valuable. In fact, Norris was not supporting agrarianism (the ranchers) v. capitalism (the railroad), but portraying economic forces at work out of pleasure in their sheer size. Ahnebrink seems to understand this when he writes, "In the clash between the farmers and the railroad he saw mainly an issue of great dramatic quality, less a social evil which should be removed" (121). This may disappoint Smrz, or Clarence Gohdes when he laments the book's "failure to indict capitalism" (753). But Norris was more concerned with proving himself—perhaps to his father—as a great and virile novelist than with promulgating any single political viewpoint.

There is no agrarianism in Annixter's remark, "We want to own our land, want to feel we can do as we blame please with it," or in Presley's reflection that the ranchers have no love for the land, wanting only "to squeeze it dry, to exhaust it" (*The Octopus* 732, 814). What may appear as a siding with the ranchers is really Norris's anti-urban stance, which is also well demonstrated in *McTeague*. Jay Martin, who feels Norris was actually rejecting his father, sees the business ethic defeating the wilderness-bred McTeague via his wife's lottery win: "the commercial success ethic, Norris suggests, debases true human ethics" (251). It is true that the novel comes close to satirizing the American dream when the lottery representative makes a long speech about how the hard-working poor—apparently never the idle rich—find happiness through winning in the scheme. But surely the creator of

Jadwin had no quarrel with the Algerist work (or success) ethic. Rather, he had sympathy with McTeague as a brute-innocent who could not (like Moran) adapt to "civilized" life.

This belief contributes to the distrust of politicians seen repeatedly in Norris's novels. If McTeague, with his strength and his animal-like "sixth sense" of danger, is one symbol of the masculine "life" side of the struggle, Norris's politicians are symbols of dressed-up, disingenuous "literature." An example is Marcus, the man who actually destroys McTeague, whom Norris invites us to laugh at as he makes half-baked political remarks like, "Decrease the number of wage earners and you increase wages, don't you? ... It's the capitalists ... that's where the evil lies" (*McTeague* 271), and later becomes secretary of the "Polk Street Improvement Club." Geary, *Vandover*'s apostle of selfishness, dreams near the end of the novel of being in Congress or the White House—and probably would have fit in there in McKinley's day.

The Octopus contains two examples of such characters: Lyman, Magnus Derrick's son, who the narrator tells us is interested only in personal power (unlike that additional grand-paternal figure, his father) and will compromise (636); and Caraher, the anarchist. The scene of Lyman's betrayal of his father is interesting because he is described as a sort of dandy, with fancy clothes and a mustache, and addresses everyone in obfuscating smooth sentences somewhat like Corthell's. "No, he had but one son," Magnus thinks as his "instincts of a father" dissolve (933), and once again, an effeminate character has been rejected by a strong male parent. Yet Lyman (a "lying-man"?), unlike his creator, does not seem to need his father's support, and is close to being elected Governor of California—a position Magnus aspired to but never achieved—at the novel's end. As for Caraher, Norris rejects both Communism and anarchy (somehow, Caraher belongs to both groups) in this character, who prods, Iago-like, Dyke and Presley toward violence with well-chosen words. His profession as a saloon-keeper also allows the moralist who had written *Vandover* to show his genteel-tradition roots again, as Presley thinks of him as "a bad man, a plague spot in the world of the ranchers, poisoning the farmers' bodies with alcohol and their minds with discontent" (1073).

Yet for all his distrust of politicians and their ideas, Norris held one political viewpoint of his own throughout his career: "the Anglo-Saxon in the course of empire had circled the globe ... March we must, conquer we must, and checked in the Westward course of empire we turned Eastward and expended the resistless energy that by blood was ours in conquering the Old World behind us" ("The Frontier Gone at Last," *Frank Norris: Novels and Essays* 1184-5). But now the conquest was through commerce, as we have seen with Cedarquist, and with Magnus Derrick's remark: "Boy, the whole East is opening, disintegrating before the Anglo-Saxon" (*The Octopus* 830). Similar passages which describe the conquest of the American West appear in both *The Octopus* and the essays. *Moran* is like a racial theory in itself. The word "Anglo-Saxon," like the word "brute," is one of Frank Norris's favorites.

Of course Norris did not create this theory. Kipling spread the same doctrine, and Le Conte may have spoken—or at least inspired—such thoughts as well. The 19th century also saw the formulation of Lombroso's theory of "criminal atavism"—an image of lesser men ruled by instinct which most likely, as Pizer asserts, influenced *McTeague* (*The Novels of Frank Norris* 57). The fact that Norris wrote a short story called "A Case for Lombroso" makes this possibility even more obvious. Like Jack London, Norris was very much a man of the time when "[f]rom Teddy Roosevelt to the common laborer, countless Americans were convinced that pure Aryan blood was somehow nobler than that of other races" (Dillingham, *Frank Norris: Instinct and Art* 56).

But this still does not excuse a man whose knowledge and sensitivity is obvious in at least his later novels. Why did he use such a belief in his fiction? Warren French, in keeping with his view of Norris as an Emersonian moralist, writes that his seeming racist statements are dynamic (the world should be improved for everybody) rather than static (we, the chosen ones, should preserve the status quo) (41). But this belief would make *The Octopus* and *The Pit* reformist rather than merely dramatic tales, and we have already seen that Norris did not consider his novels to have a "purpose." His motives in constructing a plot were that the story be big and exciting, and masculine enough in its details to make up for his feminized profession of artist. Kiplingesque racial struggles fit this latter motive perfectly.

Wars, or conquest, and such beliefs go together, of course. Dillingham wrote that Racism and Imperialism (capitalizing his themes in perhaps unconscious imitation of Norris) were the "secular gods" of the author's time in America (*Frank Norris: Instinct and Art* 87)—and they were linked to the new theory of evolution, which in the popular mind could encourage any belief about one race's superiority. Norris's pursuit of the adventure-field of war thus fits in here, and the Spanish-American War is especially relevant, because it marked the first time America extended its boundaries beyond the seas. Probably war, with its heroes and its romantic charges into the "valley of death," also appealed to Norris, as to others, by echoing ancient forms of male bonding—the army (like his college fraternity) as tribe, where the disturbing softness of women, calling toward procreation and thus individual rather than collective death, is not allowed.

The later novels may be more mature about sex, but Norris never changed his mind about race. Lynn considers him anti-Semitic, for example, and even claims that *The Octopus* is finally about America being delivered from the Jews (200). Certainly the book's villain, S. Behrman, does seem to be a stock evil Jew, a rich controller of money like Shylock, fat and swollen in appetites like the Jew of Malta. (Norris even makes an odd joke by naming Behrman's cousin, who is killed in the battle with the ranchers, Christian.) Other Jewish characters include the junk-dealer Zerkow in *McTeague*, a beast who lives in filth and has "claw-like, prehensile fingers—the fingers of a man who accumulates, but never disburses" (293); the "insignificant" Grossman, to whose trading cries nobody listens, in *The Pit*; and a nameless man who is savagely killed in *Vandover*'s shipwreck scene when he tries to climb onto a lifeboat.

The list goes drearily on. Bad dialect attempts mark comic Germanic characters in *McTeague* and *The Octopus*, and the former novel also features a half-crazed "mixed race" Hispanic woman, Maria, who marries Zerkow and gives birth to a "strange, hybrid" child which quickly dies (431). Hispanic people are also belittled in *The Octopus*, not only in the famous passage about rabbit-killing mentioned already, but in the use of the word "greaser" by the narrative voice and in Annixter's comment on Father Sarria's interest in fighting gamecocks: "There's the Spanish cropping out, after all" (740). And classism is not forgotten—recall Norris's ambivalence about "the People." Stupid, coarse servants appear in *Vandover*, *McTeague* (an absurd cook hired by Trina), *A Man's Woman* (where Bennett's orderly Adler is compared to a dog fawning on its master) (172), and *Blix*.

The alternative that the author presents to all these inferior beings is not so much the Anglo-Saxon (he's unclear on the origin of this marching race, anyway, saying "we" came from the Frisian islands in "The Frontier Gone at Last"), or even the white race generally, a group which includes that glorious descendant of Vikings, Moran. After all, a white character like McTeague can also be demeaned as bestial by Norris—and so can Vandover, a member of the author's own class, despite Geismar's claim that only the lower classes are laughed at in Norris's "survival of the wealthiest" world (23). Rather, it is a certain sort of invariably-white person, one who, whether male or female, contains the properly virile qualities of Norris's standard hero. It is a Westerner, in the sense both of European origin and area of U.S. residence.

There are several sources for the choice of this term. Lars Ahnebrink writes that the Far West was, to Norris, "inhabited by a new race, a hardy, brave, passionate, empire-building people, primitive, brutal, without fear like the West itself" (181). To this description (which has so many closely-related adjectives that it could have been written *by* Norris), Ahnebrink, a Scandinavian himself, adds the suggestion that Norse sagas and even Ibsen influenced the American author toward this view (383). And in *The Octopus*, where this idea of a new race in the West is connected to the romance-worshipper, Presley, these words appear in the same rabbit-drive scene as the passage about Mexicans: "Where else in the world were such strong, honest men, such strong, beautiful women?" (980) To Presley, there is "an honest Anglo-Saxon mirth and innocence" (979) in this strange combination of brutality and merrymaking, where women nurse their babies near the site of the rabbit slaughter.

Whatever lack of respect he shows for Presley in some scenes, Norris treats him as his personal representative in the novel in many others, and so we can assume that even these exaggerated, myopic beliefs are those of the author—particularly since he wrote several essays about the genre of Western fiction, in one calling the conquest of the West the "national epic of America" in which the already-noted "hard-grained" Americans civilized a forbidding country ("The Literature of the West," *Frank Norris: Novels and Essays* 1177, 1179). He claims also that the basic Westerner is an adventurer (as he himself wished to be), but that this chronicle should be told in a grander way than by popular dime novels. And this is exactly what *The Octopus* is meant to do.

Alfred Kazin wrote in *On Native Grounds* of Norris's "naive, open-hearted, and essentially unquenchable joy ... He was the poet of the bonanza, teeming with confidence, reckless in the face of that almost cosmological security that was California to him" (99). This is not the whole truth, since personal sorrow and guilt strongly influenced Norris's writing also, but it summarizes well how appropriate his own status as a Westerner (bred, if not born) was to the growth-drunk time in which he lived. The West made Frank Norris a perfect representative of the era which found (as he did) the conquest of the continent from Atlantic to Pacific to be both a stirring and a saddening event. Of course, his hero, or heroine, must be a Westerner. And perhaps this fact pinpoints Norris's place in the turn-of-the-century political landscape better than any other.

The Literary Norris

The final angle to Frank Norris as an individual and a representative of his time is that of the writer *as* writer—the literary background and thinking that underlies his novels. Some of this has been described already: the influence of Zola and others, the attempt of past critics to classify Norris with the naturalists or some other group. But before looking more closely in coming chapters at specific gender themes, we should fully explore the issue of how this writer, as all writers do, consciously presented himself.

As with most American artists of European descent, if we trace downward to seek the roots of Norris's artistic thought, Europe is what we find. One of his conflicts has already been shown to be the Old World v. the New—he may have enjoyed seeing himself as one of the "hard-grained, hard-riding, hard-working" army of Californians, but he also enjoyed living in Paris and coming back sporting a silk hat and a knowledge of the French language. The man whose mother had read Scott and Dickens to him could hardly expect to write outside the influence of Old World authors. And as Norris himself observed, Scott's best-known New World imitator, Cooper, was himself being imitated en masse by Americans when the 1890s began.

Clarence Gohdes gives a good description of the "prudishness" of the readers of that time, before home-grown realism burst in; though there were slums like that in Crane's *Maggie*, the average American still lived rurally.

and perhaps as ignorantly of urban poverty, at least, as Norris accused in his essay passage quoted earlier. Zola was known, and in fact popular, in America, but readers preferred to react to the naturalists with shock, and saw realism as a "hindrance to virtue." Historical romance, the exploits of knights and damsels like those of whom Norris first wrote, was most popular: "It seemed as if a dozen Fenimore Coopers were let loose all at once" (Gohdes 727, 738-9). We have seen that Norris did not conceal his disdain for Cooper, but this escapist-romantic literature remained a major influence on his own writing.

Other authors who have been mentioned in discussions of Norris include Richard Harding Davis—who had his own theme, Ziff claimed, of the "gentleman" as "the superior brute" as seen in Norris's *Moran* (265)—and even Homer, in Leonard Lutwack's view of *The Octopus* which compares its characters to specific Homeric heroes, like Annixter to Achilles (27). And Dickens had his place, too. Many have seen his influence in the typed characters of *McTeague*, Old Grannis and Miss Baker, but Norris could also create characters who were outwardly simple, but also amusing and revelatory of the human condition, just as the British master did. Broderson in *The Octopus* is prone to fall into mumbling monologues in which he constantly corrects himself, somewhat like a male Mrs. Nickleby; Blix's father is similar. Ellis, Vandover's partner in vice, who constantly quotes his sheaf of facts and statistics in order to seem knowledgeable, is another character whose repeated actions resonate beyond the mere predictability of Old Grannis's book-binding passion.

The writing class of Lewis Gates at Harvard also had its impact. Norris never quite transcended the Berkeley teacher's judgment of him as both very good and very bad; Marchand is correct in writing that the faults of his style "are but the excess of its virtues" (175). But the increasingly positive comments of the Harvard readers (rarely Gates himself) of his student themes show that his faults might have been less controlled without this class. In his introduction to the book which collects these themes, *A Novelist in the Making*, Hart quotes the Harvard catalogue as calling realism, the "habitual observation of life," the thrust of Gates's course. Only five men got an A in it, as did Norris; Gertrude Stein in the women's course actually got a C (14, 15-6).

The themes of these student assignments tend to turn up in the novels—Norris, we already know, never worked much harder than he had to. Names are traded around in early versions of *McTeague* and *Vandover*, but parts of these novels and *Blix* appear with clear individuality. The autumn of the course year belonged more to *Vandover* and *Blix* (the heroine's naughty siblings Snooky and Howard are described, for example), but *McTeague* dominated the winter, which featured a description of the massive dentist much like the novel's first page and a full plot summary (*A Novelist in the Making* 82, 88-9). Only the ugly points of the marriage, not its happy years, are described by Norris here, and his faculty reader is often disgusted. This reminds us of the young man's immature pleasure in violence. But what is most significant is the strong observation of detail in these themes—exactly as Gates, or even Dickens, would have approved—in, for example, the "Dental Parlors" description and the evocation of San Francisco in *McTeague*, or the excellent description of the Imperial restaurant later to appear in *Vandover*. Though a few critics think of his *Wave* years as an important apprenticeship for Norris, his real training seemed to have already happened by then.

But when we think of Frank Norris in terms of other writers' influence, we always return to Zola. Though Americans classed as naturalists generally refused to be as pessimistic as their mentor demanded, they were not alone in this; Zola himself could not keep to the pure requirements of his own theory. Walcutt also saw that Zola's own desire for reform (like Norris's) made his novels something other than a cold presentation of a determinist world. The Frenchman, following new medical theories, wanted fiction to be a science, but as Walcutt points out, "naturalism does not account for spirit, imagination, and personality. A work that was perfectly controlled by the theory of materialistic determinism would not be a novel but a report" (24).

The immigration of naturalism across the Atlantic made it even less doctrinaire. The tradition of "romantic individualism" which Pizer has described made Americans more interested in discovering "the validity of the human enterprise" (*Realism and Naturalism* 13) than in dissecting heredity. Walcutt observed much the same thing, and his "spirit, imagination, and personality" are three elements that certainly appear in the works of Norris, a writer who—though he may have felt less than free himself as his parents pulled him toward their own respective goals—could not by nature accept determinism. He championed Dreiser's *Sister Carrie*, but as French plausibly suggests, he "must have been disturbed ... that Carrie's wickedness went unpunished; moreover, Dreiser's stricter determinism must have clashed with Norris's notions about the ultimate triumph of good" (30). Even Ahnebrink, who sees Norris as a naturalist, finds fatalism (irrational chance ruling events, as in the lottery win in *McTeague*) rather than determinism (environment and heredity controlling man's behavior) often occurring in the novels (197-8). And though Norris tried to be like Zola in doing careful research for many of his plots and denying imagination, the youthful American optimism symbolized for him by the West and its conquest dominated his writing instead. Thus *McTeague* begins with a well-detailed evocation of milieu, what Norris called "the little life of Polk Street" (402), and two attempts at presenting characters doomed by heredity (McTeague through his alcoholic father and Trina, unbelievably, through a supposedly Central European parsimony), but becomes less realistic and more fanciful as it goes on, until it ends in the totally romantic setting of the huge Californian mountains and deserts, complete with a mysterious Indian and a prospector who all but cries, "Thar's gold in them thar hills!" (Actually, "There's gold in them damn

Panamint Mountains.") (540)

Still, critics long tried to see Norris as a doctrinaire naturalist. Marcosson called him essentially a reporter, documenting true-to-life facts in *McTeague* and *The Octopus* (78); Marchand, supporting such a view, tells us that the author always carried a notebook in which he recorded vivid images he'd seen (182). Real-life stories provided the basis for many of his novels. The trial of a San Francisco laborer who murdered his wife when she refused him money inspired *McTeague*; the sources for *The Octopus* have already been told, but Don Graham has found news stories that he believes inspired even smaller details like the sheep massacre and S. Behrman's death by suffocation in wheat (67); and the wheat-corner attempt by Joseph Leiter in 1897 was an exact parallel to Curtis Jadwin's. Above all real-world sources of plots was Capt. Joseph Hodgson, a classic salty-sea-dog of San Francisco who furnished many of *Moran*'s and *A Man's Woman*'s events—a fact which Norris himself fictionalizes when *Blix*'s "Captain Jack" tells a long yarn to Condy which he then writes up and submits to New York as a novel. Walker quotes Captain Jack as saying of *Moran* that they "wrote the book together" (162), and indeed Norris dedicated the novel to him, as he did *A Man's Woman* to the doctor who furnished its medical details.

These facts point to a curious conclusion: that the man who so exalted "life" over "literature" went to literature, i.e. stories written and told by others, much more than to "life" as a source. Despite his efforts in the two wars, Frank Norris was not a "Captain Jack"—he never lived anything like the virile tale into which he plunged his surrogate in *Moran*, Ross Wilbur, nor even witnessed or attempted violence like his surrogate in *The Octopus*, Presley. John C. Sherwood's article on the Polar voyage which contributed to *A Man's Woman* gives quotes from the journal of the commander of the real-life ship, the *Jeannette*, that are almost exactly like the passages from Bennett's journal in the novel. Though Hodgson knew the details of this expedition, the ship's journal was published and could have been read by Norris or anyone. The difference, Sherwood tells us, is that Norris let his commander survive (unlike the real-life commander) to become the expedition's, and the subsequent love-story's, only hero (251). The true story, interestingly, was also "brutalized" by Norris cutting all details but those of suffering and adding a scene in which Bennett leaves a weak crewman to die.

This use of writing as both source and plot element is a reminder of Barbara Hochman's view in *Frank Norris, Storyteller* that story-telling is a central theme for Norris. In *Blix*, the lovers even tend to treat real life as a story, manipulating it through writing in their matchmaking of Captain Jack and K.D.B.—in effect creating characters out of real people when they write notes signed with the prospective couple's names. (Condy's comment: "Why, it will be a regular drama. Only we are running the show, and everything is real.") (165) And just before the scene in which their literary matchmaking succeeds, they go fishing and find a snake trying to swallow a frog—the one thing to make that outing "perfect." Again life is like a "drama" to them, the frog's escape the "triumph of virtue," a literary construct (184). (Why didn't they try to save this flesh-and-blood frog themselves?) Similarly, that parader of masculine confrontation of "life," Frank Norris, was actually so literary in mind that he thought a scene in one story of a falling market he was told while researching *The Pit*—a crushed broker desperately echoing the word "down" spoken by an elevator rider—was the best detail, "one of those things no novelist could invent!", although it was in fact imaginary (Bixler 116).

If the use of such second-hand impressions of life went against Zola's experimental method, Norris compensated Zola by using *his* literature as a source as well. Several critics, particularly Ahnebrink, show convincing plot parallels between the French and American writers' novels. But this writer who succeeded in being viewed as a naturalist for so long never convincingly followed any tenet of naturalism. Once he even seems to laugh at the ideas he tried to use in *McTeague*, when Annixter says that he hates sticky sauce because such distaste is "in my family ... It's—it's—it's *heredity*" (*The Octopus* 675). And as for Zola's image of a detached, scientifically-objective author, it was slaughtered by the furiously lecturing narrator of *McTeague* and *Vandover*. For naturalists, the brute/spirit split presented in these novels did not exist—there was simply Norris's "brute," the animal instincts of man. Critics like Stanley Cooperman who saw this duality could explain the sentimentality and romance in American naturalism; if even Zola could not avoid the human issue of morality, Norris hardly even tried.

And yet the amoral celebration of brute instinct in *Moran* and elsewhere also exists, and reminds us of why the young Norris found the Frenchman, with his stories of large, clashing forces and often primeval behavior, enticing. Norris understood plotting much better than philosophy, and ultimately, what he took most from the seminal naturalist was not his theories but his literary techniques—especially a delight in big scenes full of people, like the barn dance in *The Octopus*, the public farewell to Bennett at the end of *A Man's Woman*, and the mad, crowd-crushing scene of Jadwin's final defeat in *The Pit*. Norris was good at such scenes, delighting as he did in bigness itself. As Ernest Marchand saw, the author "was more enamored of 'effects' than of philosophical consistency" (90).

This is probably why he imitated the naturalists. Always wishing his fiction to seem virile, he simply found these writers exciting—or even shocking, since this adherent to the genteel tradition took an adolescent delight in tweaking and teasing that tradition at times. (This is, after all, a man who even in adulthood signed a letter with a picture of a smoking gun and the words "the Boy Zola.") (Marcosson 240) In his famous essay on "Zola as a Romantic Writer," he shows far more knowledge of such "male" effects than of naturalism itself. "Terrible things must happen to the characters of the naturalistic tale. They must be twisted from the ordinary, wrenched out from the quiet, uneventful round of every-day life, and flung into the throes of a vast and terrible drama that works itself out in unleashed passions, in blood, and in sudden death" (1107). By seeing both Zola and himself as romantic, Norris was not so much defining a true literary category as trying to define himself.

After the first two novels, he made no further efforts to present even a quasi-naturalistic philosophy. Though Norris used the word when planning the wheat series, Charles Child Walcutt is much closer to the truth in his assertion that *The Octopus*'s characters are too free and heroic, like Annixter, to be naturalistic. (And the exaggerated villainy of S. Behrman, he notes, is hardly an economic force.) (145) It is here that Walcutt coins the term "natural dynamism" to describe Norris's philosophy, and this belief in some huge, benevolent maternal power makes the author a special kind of archetype-echoing romanticist—neither a naturalist nor (though he accepted the guidance of W.D. Howells early in his career) a realist. It is no wonder, when we realize with what inconsistency and confusion he followed Zola, that those who tried to see Norris as a naturalist often judged him harshly.

Norris's lack of objectivity and his delight in extraordinary plots keep him from fitting into any familiar definition (such as Pizer's) of 19th-century realism as well. Even though he remembers his debt to Howells, as when *The Pit*'s Jadwin admires his writing and feels a special kinship to Silas Lapham, it is fitting that Norris not only must make his own businessman an inflated warrior-hero, but sometimes creates in his Laura love-plot the very type of literary romance that Howells lampoons in that novel. Romance v. realism is one of the expressions of Norris's basic conflict. This is linked to two other literary issues, style and symbolism.

Norris could not write with "*no* style" as Larzer Ziff observed, despite his noisy pronouncements such as, "Damn the 'style' of a story, so long as we get the swing and rush and trample of the things that live" ("An Opening for Novelists," *Frank Norris: Novels and Essays* 1113-4). Clearly this sentence and others like it are an effort to banish "style" to the feminine side of the life-v.-literature or romance-v.-realism struggle, the side of men like Corthell, who "passed his life gently, in the calm, still atmosphere of art, in the cult of the beautiful, unperturbed, tranquil" (*The Pit* 59). We can almost imagine Norris trying to shout his "damn the style" sentence in a sufficiently manly voice, raising a clenched fist as he glances around to see if his father is nearby. Yet what happens in his fiction is really too much style rather than too little.

If Norris had not felt the necessity to repeat and repeat his points, sometimes in the same words and sometimes in different ones—and sometimes to incredible length as in the pounding analysis of the characters' feelings in *A Man's Woman*—he would have been a better writer, and his ideas would probably not have been judged as so immature. Pizer states this point well when he writes, "When he attempts to describe or analyze mental and moral states, he scarcely seems to warrant serious attention. Yet when he creates a pictorial or dramatic equivalent of his analysis," he's good (*The Novels of Frank Norris* 44). In fact, this former painter was often excellent when creating pictures, and many examples can be given of effective sensory scenes in his novels: the descriptions of rural "Sunday repose" and the rabbit drive in *The Octopus*, and even its often-criticized scene, actually a superb one, of S. Behrman's death; of the sights and smells of the harbor, and the clashing colors of Chinatown, in *Blix*; of the gross drunkenness of Vandover and his friends in *Vandover and the Brute*. Especially noteworthy is the simplicity of *The Octopus*'s climactic scene, the fatal battle at the ditch, and its aftermath; here, Norris the war reporter describes the violence with a piercing simplicity, avoiding his usual exaggerated generalizations.

But his proneness to inflation is more common, leaving his novels something like an image painted on a balloon that becomes grotesque when the balloon is pumped up with too much air. Thus we have such style elements (noted by Marchand) as three nouns or adjectives in a row without conjunctions, excessive capital-lettered personification of ideas, and repetition of words and even scenes (185). Perhaps such repetition is an expression of naturalist characters' entrapment in determinism, as Lee Mitchell has argued in the book *Determined Fictions*—and sometimes Norris *does* effectively show the self-enclosing nature of his characters' lives in this way, as when Laura sees the grim Board of Trade building in the rain at the end of Chapter One of *The Pit*, and in almost exactly the same sentence, at the book's end as well. But we have already seen that he was essentially not a naturalist. So why are Magnus and his son Harran both described as like the Duke of Wellington, for example, this description repeated as if Norris had no idea he'd used it before? Why is the same sentence used twice, in two places in *McTeague*, to describe Old Grannis and Miss Baker finally coming together? Especially, why are words like "infinite," "resistless," "vast" and (as Marchand also noticed) "diapason," "murmur," and "bourdon" so badly overused? Norris may simply have feared that his ideas (or the words that named them) would not shout loudly enough at his readers unless they appeared again and again. Just as in his shallow judgment of Zola, he looked to a novel's prose or its plot elements for meaning rather than to its underlying themes.

His symbols were overweight, too. The engine-as-life image, for example, is used in *Vandover and the Brute* to suggest at one point that the author sympathizes with Vandover, who is crushed by this engine, and at another that he supports the political-Darwinist Geary. After Vandover loses his artistic talent, Norris effectively underlines his despair by introducing the picture of Force as "some enormous engine, resistless, relentless; an engine that sped straight forward, driving before it the infinite herd of humanity ... crushing out inexorably all those who lagged behind the herd and who fell from exhaustion" (170). Poor, pliable Vandover, who as we've seen was Norris himself with his petty vices inflated to bestiality, seems a tragic figure here. But the same nature-as-engine image is described as part of the thoughts of Geary, not in the narrative voice, later in the novel when he has triumphed so completely that he even seems to have won Vandover's former "good woman," Turner. Again, the repetition is not illuminating. Which passage did Norris write first? Was he initially trying, via Geary, to espouse naturalistic determinism, in which those who "lag behind" because of fatal heredity or environment are destroyed; or was he initially the moralist, sadly chronicling the ruination of a fallible young man like himself?

The engine returns so often that we can suspect Norris simply found its size and mechanistic power, like his "manly" plot elements, exciting. In the famous scene in *McTeague* where the dentist and Trina consummate their first kiss in a dirty subway station, the train roars over their embrace "with a reek of steam and hot air" (322). In *A Man's Woman*, Lloyd sees herself as stronger than other women, reaching out "to the great engine of life whose lever she could grasp and could control, smiling proudly"; but later, when Bennett's will is broken and he's stopped exploring, she feels as if an engine has stopped (50, 218). And the image dominates *The Octopus*, of course. As Dillingham has noticed, the scene where the train kills a flock of sheep sets up the "false contrast" which led so many to think that the novel condemned the railroad (*Frank Norris: Instinct and Art* 120-1). Norris is contrasting his harsh engine symbol with the great-maternal wheat, not the railroad with the ranchers.

And so the dialectic goes, romance and realism clashing again in this novel as elsewhere. When Presley is first described, he is said to have a "delicate and highly sensitive nature," whose "refinement had been gained only by a certain loss of strength" (*The Octopus* 583). It seems that this is Norris's most frightened picture of himself after surrendering to his mother's (the sheep's?) wishes. And what is this virility-drained poet's artistic conflict?—"On the one hand, it was his ambition to portray life as he saw it— directly, frankly, and through no medium of personality or temperament. But, on the other hand, as well, he wished to see everything through a rose-colored mist—a mist that dulled out harsh outlines, all crude and violent colors" (586).

These, of course, are what Norris saw as his choices as well. The first (realist) impulse, which he rarely achieved, sounds like a description of Zola's ideal of objectivity; the second (Romantic) one, if we remember that it was not sensitive Presley but self-consciously masculine Frank Norris who wrote these novels, describes such fanciful works as *Moran* and *The Octopus* itself, in which the mist, as we saw in Sherwood's article, dulls the *alternatives* to harshness and violence more than it dulls harshness and violence. Presley is sometimes a mouthpiece for Norris's literary credo, as when he tells the effete Annie Derrick that he's uninterested in style, and says approvingly (teeth manfully clenched) that one work is not what she calls "literature" (625). But when Norris tries to distance himself from his character in the above passage, he instead reveals the delicate poet as being more like himself than he perhaps would wish.

Frank Norris fits into Chase's view of American romance more than into either European or American naturalism. He does not have Dreiser's cold determinism, Bierce's irony, Crane's almost surrealistic bleakness, or London's savagery. Instead he has a uniquely bipolar view of large forces and what George Johnson, in defining romance, calls "over-simple eternal categories." This is seen in the "melodramatic confrontation of the forces of good and evil" in *Vandover* and the "sewer" passages in *McTeague*—so that to Johnson (and others), even the first two novels are not compatible with Zola ("Frank Norris and Romance" 53-4). What Norris wishes for is not to explore complex social issues of class and milieu, but, in Johnson's words, to fly (like Presley and Bennett as they sail away at the end of their novels) "from the hard study of the realist to the poetic insight of the romancer" (63). Johnson rejects *The Octopus*'s optimistic ending, as many critics do. But it is a much more characteristic example of Norris's thought than those who connect him with his above-named contemporaries might think. The man who sought ultimate unity in the romantic dream of California wrote five novels in which characters escape prosaic life at the end to, like the classic American adolescent Huck Finn, "light out for the territories"—not only *The Octopus* and *A Man's Woman* as noted, but *McTeague*, *Moran* (where the dead heroine finally floats off West on a boat into the sea's sexual embrace), and *The Pit*, in which the Jadwins leave harsh Chicago to go, of course, West. Only *Vandover* and the already-described ending of *Blix* avoid this pattern.

Frederic Cooper, Norris's early critic, saw the novelist's interest in romanticism as his only real fault. Realism and romanticism can both exist, he felt, but Norris tried to combine them inappropriately (304). Certainly this literary cross-breeding attempt was a project of Norris's. His essay on "Accuracy v. Truth" is nothing more than another statement of his conflict, and his effort here and in the Zola essay to achieve what one critic calls "romantic-reality" is nothing more than his familiar effort to find unity. In this essay Norris asserts that naturalism stands between romanticism and realism, and says (echoing the essay "Fiction is Selection," in which he confusingly says that real life should be a writer's source, but not *stories* from real life), "Life itself is not necessarily True" (*Frank Norris: Novels and Essays* 1140). H. Willard Reninger, in a critically forward-looking article for his time, not only creates the portmanteau term "romantic-reality" for Norris, but asserts that he was attacking rather than following naturalism. Unity (called "sincerity" by Norris when writing of literature) was indeed his goal: "*Genuine realism* and *genuine romance* are precisely the same things to Norris; they meant for him genuine truth" (Reninger 222).

Reninger sees the essays collected in *Responsibilities of the Novelist* more positively than many do; but in fact, if we accept (as someone seeking "genuine truth" might) their inconsistencies, we can see their value in giving a clearer picture of Frank Norris's mind than some of the novels. In perhaps his best-known essay, "A Plea for Romantic Fiction," Norris defines the battling categories as follows: "Romance—I take it—is the kind of fiction that takes cognizance of variations from the type of normal life. Realism is the kind of fiction that confines itself to the type of normal life" (*Frank Norris: Novels and Essays* 1166). In other words, Howsellian realism—what he calls, in a famous phrase in this essay, "the drama of a broken teacup"—is "life" and Romance is "literature," the female side of the dialectic. And indeed he personifies Romance as a woman, but not a woman like Gertrude Norris at all. "She is hail-fellow-well-met with everyone she meets, a hardy, vigorous girl, with an arm as strong as a man's and a heart as sensitive as a child's" ("Novelists of the Future," *Frank Norris: Novels and Essays* 1155). And this figure, threatening our familiar little world, "would be off upstairs with you, prying, peeping, peering into the closets of the bedroom, into the nursery, into the sitting-room" ("A Plea for Romantic Fiction," *Frank Norris: Novels and Essays* 1167). This modern muse seems to be none other than Moran, that Norse heroine who combines masculine strength with feminine charms.

It is no wonder that Norris confuses the two sides of his dialectic here, seeming to exalt romance over reality in these essays but writing near the end of *The Octopus*: "Reality was better than Romance" (1087). For what do that "hail-fellow-well-met" Moran and similar Norris heroines represent—male or female? Truth, as Reninger suggests, is more a solution to the Yin-Yang struggle than a symbol of one or the other side of it, but when Vanamee praises Presley's poem "The Toilers" by saying that it's not literature, "It is Truth" (*The Octopus* 876), it seems to be representing the male (life, realism) side. But Norris wrote that life is *not* true! The answer is that however virile he tried to make his novel-writing seem, the muse was seen by him, as by most others, as a female figure. Like his male hero, though, this heroine transcends gender. Moran, Blix, and Lloyd (and perhaps, in his eyes, Jeannette) are not mere women, but feminine personifications of art and nature, like the wheat; not mere mothers—few Norris characters are demeaned by this role, as we will see later—but "Great Mothers." The author's scrambling of literary categories is simply another form of the escape he sought in such figures.

How did the male element, i.e. Norris's father, fit into his literary self-definition? Again we remember that one solution the novelist sought for his dilemma was to call his own profession manly. Novel-writing is a "most virile" act, then, not "an affair of women and aesthetes"—one must go out into life to pursue it ("Novelists of the Future," *Frank Norris: Novels and Essays* 1155). This may describe the writing of Jack London, perhaps, but not Frank Norris. His approach to his career more often followed the "feminine" side, the side that attended to morality rather than to a Nordic-hero ideal of power. In several of the literary essays Norris contrasts money-making novelists with moral ones—the very title of the collection shows his concern with this issue. And the public-taste issue, which is itself a sort of dialectic (trust in the public's judgment v. a belief that they should be guided) is linked to this position.

The literary essays are not the only example of Norris's attempts at self-definition. Condy Rivers of *Blix* represents the author as his writing self more than any other character. For example, soon after Condy is introduced in the novel with a too-often-quoted passage naming his (and his creator's) literary mentors as diseases he's caught, there is this more revealing passage: "He 'went in' for accuracy of detail; held that if one wrote a story involving firemen one should have, or seem to have, every detail of the department at his fingers' ends, and should 'bring in' to the tale all manner of technical names and cant phrases" (114). Not only does Norris describe here his Zola-inspired belief in research, but he subtly mocks that belief—in the quote marks around two phrases, the addition of "or seem to have," and most cleverly in the use of firemen, a child's favorite amusement, as his example. One can imagine the callow Condy chasing after a fire truck along with other little boys, waving his notebook in search of "accuracy of detail."

Yet Norris himself often includes passages that do more to show off his research than add to the novel's artistic impact: precise details in McTeague's "Dental Parlors" work, almost indecipherable lines about medical instruments and drugs when Lloyd discusses a typhoid case in *A Man's Woman*, and numerical descriptions of the trading in *The Pit*. He suggests through Condy that this is an error of youth, yet he will himself use such "cant phrases" throughout his own career. Thus it's not clear whether Norris is laughing at his characters or not when they are thrilled to find mention of a 45-degree angle in a Kipling book, and when Condy thinks her observation of this detail confirms Blix as the woman for him.

There are more serious points, however. Condy alone represents Norris's humorously exaggerated image of his own immaturity before Jeannette, but any idea supported by Blix in the novel is usually an important one to the author. Thus she provides her "chum" a lesson in realist writing along with all her other improvements of him. When we first see Condy at work, he is deciding (influenced by Blix) to go see a ship carrying grain to famine-stricken India—perhaps with Presley on board?—rather than faking the ship story from a clipping, a typical hack writer's trick. But after he leaves her, he gambles all night, and must fake the story the next day after all because he has no time. Writing correctly, like not gambling, is here Norris's emblem of a man's behavior under a good "man's woman" influence.

Overall, this author's pronouncements on literature were not so much a unified theory out of which he wrote as an attempt to create a unified theory from what he'd already written. This self-definition as a writer in all its manifestations—the youthful wish to be like the excitingly shocking Zola, the later desire to justify his profession to his father—is simply another attempt by Frank Norris to transcend contradictions, to make harmony out of clashing notes.

Howells wrote in his article on Norris's death, "It is not for nothing that any novelist is born in one age, and not another" (771). Frank Norris certainly was a man of his two contrasting centuries. Far from being revolutionary, a breaker of Victorian traditions as some thought, he was mainly a 19th-century man, writing against the background of the rise of the cities and the closing of the frontier, of Emerson's belief in beneficent nature and Lombroso's belief in criminally backward men. But the 20th century may include figures whose ideas help explain Norris as well. There are many lenses through which to view an author, but it is often possible to pick up another lens, one which may never have been scrutinized before, and find a new facet—or at least another way of viewing the threads and cracks within the old facets. That is why the next chapter opens with Carl Jung.

3

The Male Element: Fathers and Sons

THE JUNGIAN analysis of Norris's works referred to earlier may strike many as being most related to his familiar archetypes the "animus and anima" because, of course, as male and female symbols, they connect to Norris's endless contrast of these two genders. But these are actually two of a number of archetypes within the self, i.e. the individual consciousness that yet represents all humanity, which Jung saw as essentially equal. Furthermore, Jung tended far more to the general than the specific, and his definition even of a single term like "anima" wavered—the anima seems to be the feminine principle, the mother, *and* the total unconscious—and in any event, contemporary psychologists have almost dismissed this familiar aspect of his thinking. So the irresistible temptation to see these two archetypes as another name for Norris's dialectic must, in fact, be resisted.

Why bring up Carl Jung, then? Because the aspect of his theories most respected by many psychologists today is the mother image—divided into two forms, the Great Mother and the Terrible Mother—which relates strikingly to Frank Norris's own maternal themes. But before we consider the issue of mothers (or fathers, as this chapter does), we should explore that of the unconscious, one of Jung's other names for the anima, and how it relates to various themes in Frank Norris's fiction.

The conscious side of the human psyche is represented by reason and science—the measurable, rational universe of Newton and Locke which has dominated throughout the industrial age, including the steam-driven, Darwin-influenced period at Norris's birth. But it is through understanding the unconscious, which Jung believed manifested itself mainly through dreams and archetypal symbols, that, in his view, the human being can best develop. This division between man's machines and nature is seen quite clearly in *The Octopus*, with its contrasting symbols of the engine and the wheat. If we see Norris's theme in this novel (and more subtly in others) in such terms, the confusion over whether he had socialist aims in writing it disappears.

As in our first chapter, this division can be expressed in almost too many ways. What Jung called "the separation of subject and object" was both a physical and inner "birth"—the separation of the mother (and the eternal mother-image) from the child (5:326). Mother (or anima) is also collective unconscious, Great Mother, Mother Nature—everything represented by the wheat in *The Octopus* and *The Pit*. Jung writes that man should live in harmony with nature, and Norris in his wheat novels suggests no less. The men (never women) who don't understand this—Magnus and his fellow ranchers who wish only to bleed the land for profit, the shouting Chicago traders who quarrel over unseen wheat like clashing armies—represent the "life" side of the dialectic, the world of businessmen like Norris's father. This view can be carried further to include the deadening impact of the city on those children of nature, McTeague and Moran, and the battle of the brutal but essentially literary Bennett (remember that he is in danger of becoming "a professor" rather than "a man") against the terrible side of nature in *A Man's Woman*.

Norris tried throughout his career to reject the maternal side of his struggle as represented by *actual* mothers, as we will see in Chapter Four with its many examples of denied motherhood in the novels. But Jung's "Great Mother" is another matter. When the battle becomes one between "natural dynamism" and the world of men, Norris always seems to cheer on the feminine side. This reminds us of the need that Jung saw, and Norris felt without quite seeing, to combine Yin and Yang rather than allow the belligerent male side, hostile to the forces of nature, to dominate. Unlike Freud, who saw the unconscious as a cesspool holding all disagreeable memories and impulses, Jung believed that the contents of the unconscious can liberate the consciousness-dominated man. Blockage of the unconscious, "like bile seeping into the blood," leads to wrong outlets like war and brutality (8:364). And again, though Jung tended too often to define the components of his theory as each other, he is clear on one connection: unconscious = feminine = mother. The mother "personifies in fact the whole unconscious ... she is the gateway into the unconscious" (8:329).

Norris's wish to reconcile his opposites in this form is seen by Pizer as the belief, in the middle novels especially, that "man must draw upon his animal past for strength, but must be guided primarily by his higher and more distinctive attribute, the human spirit" ("The Masculine-Feminine Ethic in Frank Norris's Popular Novels" 90). This restatement of the gradual exchange of the familiar "brute" theme of the first three novels for the cosmic beneficence of the wheat novels reminds us of other forms of the dialectic: thinking v. feeling, spirit v. nature, and, in Jungian terms, conscious (male) v. unconscious (female). Yin, the feminine side, in Chinese philosophy is symbolized by a cloud cover, dark, hidden, and secret. Masculine is brightness, open and active (Fenton 198). We can see Norris moving toward a greater respect for the unconscious Yin as his writing progresses.

Interestingly, Jung believed that painting, Norris's first artistic endeavor, is one way to achieve the necessary union between the two sides. In art, he wrote, "a product is created by both conscious and unconscious" (8:83)—so in this view, Norris's career choice was a way to solve his conflict rather than worsen it. But only in a very negative, external way—the divorce and disowning—did this happen; the author never felt free from his internal ambivalence, as seen in the personification of this battle as Jadwin v. Corthell in his very last novel. In fact, Jung did not mind the idea of such an eternal battle: "If they must contend let it at least be a fair fight with equal rights on both sides" (9.1:288). This is what he called the process of individuation. It is a good description of how one man, Frank Norris, carried out both his internal struggle and the larger struggle of his era-closing time in selecting the plot and character details of his novels. This selection will be examined in terms of men in this chapter, and women in the next.

Who, then, is the archetypal father? He is the denial of what the mother offers, standing in the doorway to regression and rebirth, like Marcus appearing to punish and kill McTeague after his flight into the wilderness. Like the Great Mother, the "great" father is more than the individual father; he is all of society and its rules, "the sum of conventional opinions" (9.2:15)— so it's not surprising that one commentator on Jung sees this father/animus image as simply a renaming of Freud's superego (Stevens 200). The father's archetypal role is, like the superego's, as a representative of moral law, hostile to sex (as Norris the narrator so often was), the giant who guards the treasure (5:261). And like Siegfried fighting Fafner, Norris faced this giant as best he could.

Jung liked to use the biblical phrase "sins of the father" to describe how parents' psychological difficulties were repeated in their children's lives. Is this "curse" what Benjamin Franklin Norris, Sr. bequeathed to his son? We know little about the father's character from Walker, and only somewhat more (allowing for fictional license and wishful thinking) from the relevant characters in Norris's novels. But since what the father symbolizes is, Jung asserts, more important than who he personally is, we have enough information (whether or not we fully agree with this notion) to describe the son's conflict in these terms. The "curse" is already partly invoked, whatever one's own parents are like, by the opposing archetypes themselves. The father introduces the child to society whereas the mother is (traditionally!) oriented towards the home. More significantly, while mother love is absolute, instinctive, father love is contingent love, conditioned upon performance in the world. This belief of Jung's as reported by Stevens (108-9) may not be true in many actual families, but it seems a perfect description of Norris's.

The jeweler Norris does appear, from our few pictures of him, to have been more of a society character than an intimate family one. It is easy to imagine him, like Curtis Jadwin, rarely spending time within the enclosing walls of home, preferring work and the father-figure role of teaching Sunday School. Mrs. Cressler mentions this school, and his charitable support of a Children's Hospital, as part of her "selling" of Jadwin to Laura; and later in the novel, Norris does his best to make this scheming businessman look moral when he uses his power to make the man who swindled Hargus ("poor old Hargus ... supporting his little niece, too, while you, you have been loafing about your clubs, and sprawling on your steam yachts, and dangling round after your kept women") pay his money back (*The Pit* 326). (We can recall here that part of the father's archetypal role is as a guardian of morality, and Norris tried to take this role himself when writing on the "responsibilities of the novelist.") But this image of a benevolent Richard the Lionhearted of society and business is not the image of a caring father. Jadwin expresses a condescending affection for his Sunday-school charges (whom he calls, and Frank Norris, Sr. perhaps called, "little micks"), but, like all the couples who are central in these novels, he and Laura have no children of their own. And Norris's father may well have acted as if he had none.

What love he showed probably *was* conditional. His oldest son's failures must have impressed him negatively, to the point of cutting Frank alone out of the divorce settlement. And throughout his life—in his college fraternity and his chasing after armies in hopes of male-bonding adventure—Norris tried to compensate for this lack of acceptance from that most important sharer of a son's own gender. The search for adventure was partly, as noted, an attempt to break out of his sheltered childhood life, but it was also a search for fulfillment of the ancient tribal desires of which Jung writes. A perfect illustration of this wish is the absurd scene in *Moran* where Ross Wilbur, having graduated from collegiate pranks to killing a Chinaman in a fight, is carried on the shoulders of the old Yale men in his "set," in the spirit of past "athletic triumphs," upon his return to California. "Ross was Yale, y'know," says one, "Yale '95; ain't we enough Yale men here to give him the yell?" (252).

The importance of masculinity, individual and collective, is always paramount to Norris—even when he also sought the alluring maternal archetype—because of this rejection. His love of he-man activities and plots, illuminating what Geismar calls America's "virility complex" (9), is both a response to it and a familiar form of the aggression which Jung and others see as a basic drive. This stands also behind his pro-business conservatism, his support of Anglo-Saxon conquest, and his difficulty in making female characters truly feminine. Norris's tendency to give female characters male names (Turner, Moran, Sidney, etc.) is a well-known manifestation of this latter point—and he went so far with it as to call his daughter Jeannette "Billy." His friend Juliet Tompkins writes that both parents "wanted to name the child Billy, simply because it would be such fun to call 'Billy!' and then have a little girl appear" (Foreword to *The Pit* viii-ix). But what we know of Norris's life suggests a deeper reason than fun. We recall that his masculine-woman characters were claimed by some critics to be the only ones he respected. This seems to be borne out by his making a heroine of Moran Sternerson, "the half-masculine girl in men's clothes" (*Moran of the Lady Letty* 98) who eats with her knife, drinks whiskey, and pounds the mess table with her fist. But Moran is more a very odd father-figure—replacing an earlier father-figure, Captain Kitchell, in the novel after his death—than a romantic heroine. (Her surname suggests her succeeding him as a "sterner son" than her mate Wilbur.) What Norris respected most in a woman was strength, as shown best when Lloyd masters the fever-weakened Bennett in *A Man's Woman*, and thus wins his love—a strength symbolized by the names of Lloyd and others who were equal to men.

And Gertrude Norris's son must have sensed her equality as well. Though he was angry at himself (and thus at her) for his failure to please his father, he must have had an ambivalent sense of partnership with the woman who had briefly tamed this father-giant and defeated him by making her son an artist. The double-bind made it impossible for Frank Norris to reject either parent—in fact his close relationship with Gertrude, which as we've seen continued into adulthood, may have had the sort of undue intensity which Jung calls a "secret conspiracy," through which each partner "helps the other to betray life" (9.2:11). An unsatisfactory marriage is one reason Jung suggests for a mother who tries to keep the child too close, so that his development is blocked. Norris's immaturity, derided by so many critics, was probably nothing more than a result of this bond. Thanks to Jeannette (not "Billy," but the first, totally feminine Jeannette), he broke free.

Still the image of a larger-than-life, archetypal mother that could unite his opposing sides tantalized Norris. Jung defines individuation (interestingly, the word "individual" can be said to mean "not dividable") as bringing together the conscious and unconscious (5:301). The Sanskrit word for opposing pairs, "dvandva," can mean man and woman, or (sometimes quite appropriately!) quarrel. To be untouched by opposites is the meaning of the negative of this word, "nirdvandva," which has been simplified in our pronunciation to "nirvana" (Jung 6:195). And Norris wrote often of a "second self" that shared the consciousness of his characters; for example, "that other Vandover whom he felt was his real self, Vandover the true man, Vandover the artist" (*Vandover and the Brute* 83). (At one point he even refers to *three* Vandovers, one watching the other two struggle—perhaps mother, father, and child?) Of course a wife is often called a man's "better half," which shows the universality of the split that this one man felt. What else could he have been seeking at the end of *The Octopus*, with its "larger view" free of good and evil, but what many seek—nirvana exactly as Hinduism defines it?

But the father as well as the mother was capable of bestowing great gifts; for the father-image is, of course, also a God-image. Jung makes this point often: in myth the father archetype is the King, the Father in Heaven, again the defender of the status quo (Stevens 105). One mythical god, Kronos, tried to prevent his sons from replacing him by eating them. If this suggests Frank Norris, Sr. in one light, so does the fact that God can also equal intensity and power—the libido, which is also the younger Norris's "force." All symbols, Jung thought, can be reduced to libido (5:97). But it is our reason-dominated Western society, such as in the Catholic Church with its male trinity, that is most likely to see God as male, rather than as a lovingly procreative mother-figure.

Norris gave no attention to religion in his life, however, and God as a myth-image seems more important in his books than as a personal cherisher and helper. Early in his career, in *Vandover*, he was firmly denying God. In the shipwreck scene (just before Vandover's own father dies), Van sees a Salvationist woman, who is certain that she'll be saved, instead freakishly killed by a falling piece of the ship. This scene's significance has been noted by others, but a more direct denial later in the book has gone comparatively unnoticed. After his disease (perhaps a result of syphilis, as Pizer believes, or perhaps the more mysterious ennui-fever that Jadwin also suffers in *The Pit*) gives him melancholia and insomnia, Vandover prays one night for help. But there is "no answer, nothing but the deaf silence, the blind darkness" (181). Eternal life is denied in the same paragraph.

Vandover's despair was probably a parallel to Norris's; like the loss of Van's father, this Godless-universe theme is consistent with the book's being written just as its author's own "King" was lost via the divorce. Before we assume that Norris was an atheist at this point, we must remember the "guilt, unhappiness, and insecurity" with which this novel "reeks" in Lynn's words (168). Every surrender of Vandover's to vice leaves some echo of his thought during his first collegiate drunkenness: "What *would* the governor say to *this*?" (*Vandover and the Brute* 15). After he first has sex, he writes his father asking for his forgiveness, and turns to him again after his first great crisis, Ida Wade's suicide. But after his father dies (perhaps during the very shipwreck in which Van first sees God's apparent absence), there is no more opportunity to turn to this masculine hero for comfort and repentance. Now the Judgment Day which some religions believe offers no hope of forgiveness afterward has come to Vandover as an individual—as Norris may have felt it had to him. The actual father and the archetypal father have both departed, and the constant moral lecture by an intrusive narrator is the author blaming himself for this loss.

But by the time of *The Octopus*, God had entered Frank Norris's fictional world. Alfred Kazin even sees the novel's plot as a Biblical legend, with the wheat-growing valley as Eden and the railroad as the invading serpent (100). Norris's set of symbols in the book do not, however, suggest that the author had such a plan in mind. What he did have was a God-in-all-things view which again reminds us of Emerson, as well as standard religion personified by Father Sarria and his sermons on immortality to Vanamee (who later speaks St. Paul's line, "Oh, grave, where is thy victory?"). Annixter thinks of Hilma as God's gift to him, and Presley looks at the wheat growing in its "colossal power ... alone with the stars and with God" (934)—but it is a more direct statement of Norris's theology here to say that the wheat *is* God. It even personally kills the villain, S. Behrman, at the book's end ("Vengeance is mine; I will repay, saith the Lord"). This is the opposite of Christianity, which since St. Augustine has generally seen divinity as non-physical, even anti-physical; it's a shamanistic belief in God as everywhere in nature.

The middle novels are not as clear a transition here as they are in the issue of sex. The first two present worlds of simple animal pleasure in which no God seems necessary, and only in *A Man's Woman*, when the narrator asserts that "God had made [Bennett] for" the "terrible work" of polar exploration, does the King really appear (208). The presentation of the male *ubermensch* Bennett as a tool of God's will returns us to the view of a force-wielding divinity that Norris (and all of us, if we believe in Jung's archetype) identified with his father.

Critic Oscar Cargill made early use of the term "superman" in describing McTeague, and also called Jadwin "the most plausible superman" of Norris (106). He also mentioned Nietzsche in connection with both Moran and Bennett. Norris's connection to the German writer is unclear, and has not been asserted as a true debt even by Lars Ahnebrink, who connects so many European writers with American naturalists. But the force of will and power that he emphasizes in connection with all these characters—though they are very different, McTeague a brainless animal, Bennett intelligent but animal-like in moral code, and Jadwin a fully human, consciously moral hero—makes the word "superman" not inappropriate. This description of Bennett is typical: "a force and a power of mind that stopped at nothing to attain its ends, that chose the shortest cut, the most direct means, disdainful of hesitation, holding delicacy and finessing in measureless contempt, rushing straight to its object, driving in, breaking down resistance, smashing through obstacles with a boundless, crude, blind Brobdingnag power, to oppose which was to be trampled under foot upon the instant" (*A Man's Woman* 91).

Even in *A Man's Woman*, where Norris tends to belabor his points, there are few passages so prolix and hammering as this one. Does this emphasis show that Norris was describing the kind of man (since "disdainful of hesitation ... rushing straight to its object" hardly described the author's own will) he truly admired? Perhaps not, because he is almost as repetitive when describing Bennett's weakness after he becomes ill and surrenders to Lloyd. As with the portrayals of Jadwin and Shelgrim, there is an ambivalence here which suggests again that, unless Norris's male hero has some "Yin"-side qualities as well, he is an imperfect being. It is only the superman or Godlike man that we see as a father figure in these novels, never the "wise old man," such a familiar character in myths and tales of magic, who Jung tells us is an important archetype. Norris's heroes are strong rather than wise ones, like the Homeric warriors Leonard Lutwack mentions, or the Norse-saga brute Grettir.

However Norris tries to make someone like Jadwin his hero, he is still enticed by the mythical standard of a *younger* (son, rather than father) hero—someone who slays, rather than is, the dragon, who wins the woman in the end. Annixter, who faces the power of the railroad as well as besting the cowboy Delaney in a man-to-man gunfight, is thought of by Hilma as "a hero who stood between them all and destruction ... He was her champion" (*The Octopus* 836). Earlier, Norris compares him to famous literary heroes. By contrast, Bennett, with his "inexorable bestial determination," who treats his expedition's men as "his serfs, his beasts of burden, his draught animals, no better than the dogs straining in the traces beside them" (*A Man's Woman* 11-12), is, like Shelgrim, a commanding father rather than a classic son-hero. Norris leaves no doubt that his single-minded determination saves his and his men's lives in the Arctic, but in civilization, he (like McTeague and other Norris men) is completely inept when confronted with a woman. What we are seeing in these characters is not the ideal man, but images of a stern, towering parent from the point of view of a little boy.

So this search for heroes, like that of Presley as he tries to write an epic, does not turn up standard epic heroes. In part they may be "supermen," but Bennett is also described by George Johnson as an "adult Boy Scout" ("The Frontier Behind Frank Norris's *McTeague*" 102)—a slightly more mature version of the boy introduced to male tribalism via knots and camping knives. At the beginning of *A Man's Woman*, Bennett believes that his masculine will is enough to defeat Mother Nature. This is one definition (but not the full definition) of the "Enemy" he and Lloyd endlessly face in the book—an Enemy with whom, in the early Arctic-march chapters, Bennett sees as being in "a battle without rest and without end and without mercy" with himself. Thus he melodramatically shakes his fist at the ice, and writes in his journal: "Succeed I must and shall" (9, 14). But the Mother is stronger than one man, and as a joke, she makes the ice drift northward so that all his marching south leaves him and his men farther north than a month before.

Jay Martin notes that other male characters, like Magnus and Jadwin, have greatness "measured precisely in terms of their ability to compete with immutable laws" (73)—they, too, both fail to conquer the Great Mother (in this case the wheat), but their mere efforts against such a towering figure make them great. Another way to view this is that any man who loses in competition with feminine "immutable laws" must recognize the strength of the mother. Magnus tries greedily to bleed the land for profit, and Jadwin to control the wheat in the Pit, but both are in error, and both, at the end of their respective novels, fittingly surrender to the sheltering arms of their wives.

Because of such details, we must wonder whether Norris is cheering along with the rest of America when Bennett returns from his mission. Lloyd's manifesto of force, spoken to her man's comrade-in-arms Ferriss, is the sort of speech that makes some misunderstand the novel: "The world wants men, great, strong, harsh, brutal men—men with purposes, who let nothing, nothing, nothing stand in their way" (*A Man's Woman* 71). Of course this is not what the world wants, we have learned since; we got such men in the 20th century and they caused wars and genocide. But is Norris really ignorant of this danger? He spends most of the second half of the novel teaching Bennett that trying a "great, strong, harsh, brutal" stance against the civilized world of women does not work. After Ferriss's death, caused by Bennett's refusal to let Lloyd nurse him, the broken hero admits a possible mistake to himself for the first time. He has lost his "arrogant and vast self-confidence," and why?— because, as with McTeague, "a woman had entangled herself in the workings of his world" (167).

Norris's view of masculinity, particularly in his later novels, was thus not as simple as many think. And the germ of this new view was his ambivalence toward his father, now that his parents' marriage had ended. Now, power becomes foolishness rather than virility, and business activity is presented less as sheer heroism and more as gambling. This vice, seen directly in Vandover and Condy's behavior in earlier novels, is symbolic in the wheat books; Magnus, a poker player, is generally described as a gambler— "He was always ready to take chances, to hazard everything on the hopes of colossal returns" (*The Octopus* 61)—and Jadwin's speculation is at bottom nothing more than attraction to the same vice. Norris makes this obvious with bits of irony like Jadwin's refusal to bet on a pool game, or his flipping a coin to decide whether to act on his first insider-tip.

Gambling is a vice with which the author seems to have sympathy, however. Magnus's wish for a "Chance" to grab is an ironic one in the light of Norris's fatalistic motif—the constant play of chance, usually negatively, on characters' lives, as when Trina McTeague wins the lottery. Also, the selfish character Geary shrewdly refuses to gamble in *Vandover*, while the novel's half-helpless hero is taken in. Norris understood the temptation to shuffle money as in his father's world—what is called, after Condy's release from gambling in *Blix*, the "artificial world" of men (228). Condy, instead of remaining dry and colorless as the narrator describes him when in the grip of "the one indomitable, evil passion of the man" (this man or any male?) (152), becomes more ambitious and energetic with the aid of his woman. Again we see in this symbol of immorality Norris's mingled distaste and desire for the masculine sphere in life.

However imperfect, though, these paternal heroes with their "salient" jaws (it was Marchand who noticed the overuse of this word) and their inflated power always symbolize one of Norris's most common themes: that of "force." This is the libido of Jung's male God-image. Another name the psychologist gives this is "psychic energy," to distinguish it from Freud's merely sexual notion—the "primordial creative principle," seen in a number of myths (5:138). Jung does not reject the term "libido," but he sees the word as embodying far more than sex, or life-force, for that matter. The Hindu term "rta," which means established order, destiny, divine law—all that a paternalistic deity might impose—is the creative principle, the libido, to Jung (6:208). (An Arabic word of similar meaning, "haqq," is used in the Koran.) And Jung identifies "rta" in turn, fittingly enough, with the Chinese "tao" (the way), which is exactly what is divided into Yin and Yang.

Force is not always Norris's answer to the dialectic—not in the mouth of Shelgrim, for example, who is a wholly masculine figure. But when it is divine force or "rta," as in the organic fertility of the wheat—what Pizer calls "beneficent cosmic determinism," the teacher of Annixter and Vanamee (*The Novels of Frank Norris* 140)—it is powerful enough to create such uniting optimism as that which ends *The Octopus*. It is something other than the overweight, capitalized forces, like the "Enemy" of *A Man's Woman*, that Norris wrote of before the wheat novels, something appearing fully only in the last two years of his life after his marriage. The Chinese "tian" (heaven), itself connected to tao, resembles Norris's wheat as an impersonal sacred power which can reward and punish. Tao also reminds us of *The Octopus* with its division into Yin-Yang seasons of cold and dry, growth and harvest (Fenton 198).

.   Perhaps the early attempts to follow Zola hindered Norris's development of this theme of order-granting power. Jung himself comments on naturalism that its view of a "constant 'downward' tendency" in the instincts denies the divine-law creativity which *is* nature. "The natural flow of libido ... means complete obedience to the fundamental laws of human nature, and there can positively be no higher moral principle than harmony with natural laws that guide the libido in the direction of life's optimism" (6:212-3). It practically seems as if the psychologist is stating the theme of *The Octopus*. Norris was rarely more wrong than when predicting that his wheat novels would be "straight naturalism."

        Thus when Presley finally believes only in "primordial energy," thinking that "[m]en were naught, death was naught, life was naught; FORCE only existed" (1084), we are in one of the passages where Norris does not agree with his alter-ego. He is still under Shelgrim's spell, and must be taught the true nature of the creative force by Vanamee: "Never judge of the whole round of life by the mere segment you can see. The whole is, in the end, perfect" (1086). It is far from coincidence that on this same page we see what Jung feels represents the male libido-power most strongly, when the next morning, "the sun moved over the edge of the world and looked down upon all the earth like the eye of God the Father." Oscar Cargill is right to laugh at Presley's duping by Shelgrim—"One is to suppose that thereafter [he] never ate a meal without considering his mashed potato as a force and his fork as a force" (104)—but wrong to think Norris is duped as well. Tutored by the mystic Vanamee and shined upon by the most powerful of masculine symbols, Presley overcomes his bewilderment and learns that the massive businessman's vision was limited.

        This is far from the image of force as a relentless engine in *Vandover* years before. From this novel, and the brutal *McTeague*, we progress to Norris's chiding Bennett for his approach to life that is so forceful he finds he can't control his *own* force (*A Man's Woman* 173), to the wheat, "that gigantic world-force, that colossal billow, Nourisher of the Nations" (*The Pit* 357). Jadwin even thinks of the wheat as tumbling over him like an ocean, as it did to S. Behrman—and water images, of course, are female. The harsh masculine force of a man like Bennett has been replaced by something quite different.

Water, where life on earth began, is a fertility symbol, and light or the sun a libido-symbol (Jung 5:315). The womb is also watery, of course, and return to the womb equals immortality. Jung unites these symbols by pointing out that the sun both rises and sinks into the water (5:216), so that birth and death are blended by the two genders. *Moran* is the novel of Norris's most relevant to these images, since it is dominated by the ocean, the kindly mother: "Never to Wilbur's eyes had the Pacific appeared so vast, so radiant, so divinely beautiful" (38). But the sun symbol appears as well, as the ship of Captain Kitchell, the novel's original father-figure, is described once as sailing on the ocean "alone with the sun" (106). This same sun is "flogging" Moran and Wilbur, like a punishing parent, after their fatal fight with the Chinamen.

Another Norris theme, bigness, connects to this worship of large or heavenly forces. It has been noted that largeness of effect was probably the main thing attracting the American to Zola; his character Presley, too, is intoxicated by immensity and the "colossal power" of the wheat. Again and again Norris mentions great size in his descriptions, or uses the word "infinite." McTeague's most common words of anger are that someone is "making small" of him, and at the novel's end, he escapes into nature's immensity, as Blix and Condy do when they roam by the open Pacific. Norris may have written of such large horizons because he felt small or entrapped himself—always, at least until his marriage, the child looking up at the two forceful figures arguing over whose mold would shape him. No wonder Jadwin is described as being fully twice the size of the "slightly built" Corthell (*The Pit* 15, 30).

Ironically, Norris was himself, like a Zola character, partly doomed by heredity. A further exploration of his life, with a focus on this inheritance of the "sins of the father," provides a bridge to our examination of the male figures in his novels.

Norris, Sr. and Norris, Jr.

Jung wrote that "when animus and anima meet, the animus draws his sword of power and the anima ejects her poison of illusion and seduction" (9.2:15). These overweight symbols for the battle of the sexes remind us of how violently Norris often saw the same issue—for example, in the two doomed marriages depicted in *McTeague*. His parents' ultimately failed marriage may have often reached the level of sword v. poison as well, and the hardening of his father's will in response to this conflict had a strong impact on the son and on the son's novels.

It is little wonder that this man so often called boyish or naive wished to remain a boy for so long. The failures of his childhood already explored—the football attempt, Paris, the weakness in school that led him, in the voice of the character Adler, to condemn Bennett for considering a "professor" career, and finally the divorce and disinheritance—add up to a recipe for despair. For a time he tried to deny adulthood, and a man's necessity to face, through marriage and parenting of his own, his replacement and thus loss of his father. The comic-book adventure plots of the short stories and *Moran*, and his own confused, fever-ridden adventures in South Africa and Cuba, are examples of this denial. But, contrary to what many critics write, Frank Norris did grow up. After the battles and starvation he saw in Cuba, he wrote that "there is precious little glory in war" (quoted in Walker 214), and the novel written after this experience, *A Man's Woman*, is the first one to recognize that brute force is not the way to meet life.

Flight and return, as Glen A. Love points out, is one of the battles in Norris's works. Though he wrote, as seen already, many escapist endings, there was also an understanding that flight is not always possible; thus we know, although it's not stated in the book, that Wilbur returns to his ordinary "taxpayer" life after the death of Moran (herself certainly a creature not only of seduction, but of illusion). McTeague's flight ends in his death, and Bennett's return to the Arctic is more a confrontation of the forces he had grown to fear than a truly romantic escape. Warren French believes that Norris "could only advise flight" (105), but there is a mature facing of the author's own past in his later novels that denies this. In the end, by returning to his birthplace of Chicago both in life, to research *The Pit*, and in the setting of that novel, Norris was accepting return.

What was he confronting in this novel? The character of Jadwin, as we've seen, was treated with much uncertainty. This attempt to create the ultimate businessman-hero, the capitalist as warrior in Smrz's "amoral romance," often reveals him as, in the Czech's words, a "big, overgrown boy blundering through situations that call for a mature, self-controlling man," another Babbitt (70). Jadwin is life-size, not a Shelgrim, because Norris always had his father, about whom he must have felt great ambivalence, in mind when he wrote his novel. This character, like Norris's other men, will be examined more closely in the next section. What is important here is the series of life-experiences, and the emotions they caused, which led to this ambivalence in the writer's fiction.

The flight from responsibility which French saw may not occur so openly in Norris's novels, but the temptation to it certainly does. This wish for freedom from civilization, as seen in *Huckleberry Finn*, is one of the aspects of Frank Norris that mark him clearly as an American writer. But while Huck and Tom saw a world of women as the thing to flee from, Norris equated civilization more with men, exemplified by the business-building father who proudly labelled himself a "capitalist" and wished his son to do the same. It was the female side of his dialectic, symbolized by California and his own definition of romance, to which Norris and his characters wished to escape.

For this reason, we have his persistent theme of the city as evil. Born in Chicago, Norris seemed to wish to apologize, just like Condy, that he "couldn't help that, you know" (*Blix* 114). From the beginning, the urban world of his father threatens and destroys Norris's characters. In *Vandover*, even feminine San Francisco is revealed, through the triumph of Geary, to be what French calls "an unnatural place where the innocent suffer, the susceptible go astray, and the corrupt flourish ... Virtue means nothing here; the prize goes to the technically competent" (60). Certainly the words "susceptible" and (despite the condemning narrator) "innocent" describe Vandover well, and Norris seems to offer him hope only in his first adult home, whose setting with chickens, cows and a windmill in the yard is described at length. Soon after this description, however, we are introduced to the sordid urban restaurant, the Imperial, whose nature would be obvious enough without Norris's additional symbols of a witches' sabbath picture over the bar and a "showcase full of live snakes" in a drugstore nearby (*Vandover and the Brute* 32-3). This is where Vandover will seduce Ida Wade, one of the chief steps downward in his fall.

McTeague repeats this theme through the failures of a variety of characters. While Love argues that Norris is not really exalting the natural world against the city, he also chooses the perfect words to describe this "mythic American pattern of rejection of the threatening metropolis," as McTeague, Trina's family and Marcus, all "inept urbanites," try and fail to build lives beyond San Francisco. The end in Death Valley actually punctures the frontier myth, since the cowboy and the miner fumble away their chance for survival by shooting the water-carrying mule (Love 10, 14). *Moran*, whose heroine says of San Francisco, "And people can live there, good heavens! Why not rabbit-burrows, and be done with it? ... I hate this place" (274), illustrates this theme most simply, as Moran is killed shortly after her ship reaches the city. She is not, like McTeague, a child of nature rendered unable to survive in the wild by his urban years, but a child of nature unable to survive for more than a day in civilization at all. The almost Edenic beach in Mexico where she and Wilbur play the roles of innocently bestial man and woman is her real home; and the ocean and sunset descriptions of the couple's first "beautiful" evening there (169) remind us of the city-escape scenes in *Blix*.

This novel seems to mark a change with its presentation of the city as a playground for lovers, but the open Pacific gives them, like Moran and Wilbur, the most pleasure. "We might be a thousand miles away from the city," says Blix happily as they walk along the beach (231); and it is in this setting that Condy realizes his love for her. The country surroundings where Lloyd takes her holiday in *A Man's Woman* are described more fully and positively than the unnamed city where she works. And in *The Octopus*, city-bred Lyman turns corrupt; Hilma cries in her hatred of the "crude, raw" city when she runs to San Francisco after Annixter's lewd proposal (896-7); and the Hooven family is finally destroyed, the mother dead of starvation and the older daughter a prostitute, when they go to the same city and face "the hard, huge struggle of city life" (1030).

In Jung's theories, the creation of cities has replaced primitive tribal ties, which themselves had replaced the severed relationship with the mother (8:373). Cities leave man totally alienated. Norris never lived successfully outside the city himself, and constantly sought, as in his fraternity days, the sort of relationship to which the psychologist refers. The Great Mother to which McTeague tried to flee, which became instead the hellish desert of Death Valley, turned her face away from Frank Norris in the wilderness as well—giving him only fevers which ironically, via his appendicitis, killed him just when he was planning to buy his own Magnus-Derrick-style ranch. What he was left with in his lifetime was an existence on his father's ground, in which he tried unhappily to succeed according to his father's standards.

Never able to make a choice in the art v. commerce struggle, belittling and yet identifying with characters like Corthell, Norris wished to deny his father's world even as he courted it. We've seen that one critic, Jay Martin, thinks commercial values are condemned in *McTeague*; and Walter Benn Michaels points out that both Trina's miserliness and Vandover's spendthrift nature are an attempt to deny the value, and thus the power, of money (143-4). Trina "spends" her gold on itself—on the sheer physical pleasure of owning it—not to produce an income or for food. And fittingly enough, all her gold ends up in the middle of the desert, beside her dead husband, where nobody can spend it (Michaels 141, 150). The role of money as a sexual surrogate in the novel has been noted often, and William Freedman's Freudian article on *McTeague* sees this as a social comment, too: "Money has become her lover as it is her society's" (57). Furthermore, she gains the power through money that she cannot gain over her man physically, as when she wins an argument by telling him, "Who's got the *money*, I'd like to know?" (*McTeague* 454).

Kenneth Lynn writes that Norris "suffered all his days from having been born with a silver spoon in his mouth" (160)—implying that he felt guilty about or weakened by his sheltered upbringing—but the truth is probably more subtle, that the author was angry at his own temptation by the money he needed (and failed) to prove himself worthy to inherit. Thus, even though he made the businessman his hero, the city as a representative of mercantilism, or even money itself, was negatively presented in his novels.

Perhaps his weakness with figures was an unintended rebellion against the same thing. The collegiate dilettante who never passed his math exam is later revealed, just like his character Vandover, as able to do sums when they're important to him. When Vandover is finally stricken with poverty, he loses his confusion with figures and works out in detail how to live on $5.75 a week. Similarly, Norris is uncharacteristically (we assume) precise in figuring out the income and expenses of a novelist as money-maker in one literary essay. His perhaps unconsciously-motivated failure in youth seems a more likely source for guilt feelings than the mere fact of having been born privileged. His celebration of mindlessness may be an effort to make this failure seem morally correct.

In any event, it was only in his first twenty-four years, before his disowning, that Norris never finished anything (e.g. Berkeley, his Paris art studies); starting with the Harvard year, he achieved everything he wished, including the production of the industriously researched *The Octopus* and *The Pit*, with one notable exception—his attempts to be a "man" like his father by going to war. It is true that he could not write for a time in 1897, but after a visit to the Placer County mining country (the Great Mother of immense nature) where *McTeague* ends, he finished *McTeague* and was successful in writing all of his later novels. (Fittingly, Condy Rivers needs the prodding of a more flesh-and-blood woman, Blix, to overcome his lack of ambition and further his writing career.)

But if the "secret conspiracy" between Norris and his mother seems to have succeeded after 1894, the son still remembered the father. Rescued by his own fortuitous failures from becoming a second-generation jeweler, Frank Norris, Jr.—who never used the "Jr." in his writing bylines—was now, in the bloom of adulthood, making a sufficient living in the world of literature instead. It is not only the persistence of characters like Cedarquist and Jadwin, however, that provide a clue to his continuing double-bind. Even the essays collected in *The Responsibilities of the Novelist* are a plea to his father for understanding.

Some critics think there is no logical underlying idea in this collection, and certainly some of it simply reflects Norris's need to fill his money-making magazine columns. Others, like William B. Dillingham, see a definite center to the essays, mostly written in the final years of Norris's life. Did he write them because he "needed to state his creed," to keep himself from straying out of a defined literary standard? (Dillingham, *Frank Norris: Instinct and Art* 45). Certainly we've seen that his wish to name himself an adherent of Romance was one motivation. But Kenneth Lynn sees the essays' image of the responsible novelist as addressed to the Sunday-school-teaching father who admired Dwight Moody, and the essays' general ideological thrust as pro-capitalist (185-6). Norris may not have been happy to write such ideas, however. If "the subversion of art by economic power" is one theme of *Vandover* (Graham 28), it is a theme of the literary essays as well; and Norris's familiar ambivalence is a good explanation here as elsewhere for the inconsistencies some have decried.

In an essay revealingly titled "The True Reward of the Novelist," Norris writes angrily of fiction-writing perverted by novelists who are mere "businessmen": "They find out ... what the public wants, and they give it to the public cheap, and advertise it as a new soap is advertised ... they make money; and if that is their aim ... let's have done with them" (*Frank Norris: Novels and Essays* 1147). Then let's "have done" with Frank Norris, we could argue, because he tried to do the same in his middle novels at least; his awareness of genre is clear in all three of them. *Moran*, it is revealed in Norris's letters of the time, was not only written with commercial tastes in mind, but with hardly any clear outline. Norris was writing rapidly for serialization, and did not even decide that Moran should die until he reached the novel's end. *Blix* was even more conventional than the (as Debra Munn describes it in her article on *Blix*) "wild but saleable" *Moran*; it was published in a magazine for women called, fittingly enough, the *Puritan*, "and a single reading clearly indicates that Norris designed the story with such a readership in mind" (Munn 47). As for the subject of *A Man's Woman*, Pizer points out that Arctic exploration "was as much a matter of public interest in the late 19th century as space exploration is today" (*The Novels of Frank Norris* 103).

Knowing this does not require us to condemn Norris, of course, as he condemns venal novelists, but simply to see that on this issue, too, he was torn by ambivalence. Are novelists who are "businessmen" evil? But a businessman is what Norris's father wanted him to be, and the essays in *Responsibilities of the Novelist* sometimes read like a plea that he has achieved this role—or at least is more masculine in it than any Presley-like poet. The essay in which he shows how a novelist can make a profit has already been mentioned. And in the title essay, he lays out yet another dialectic by saying that "vital interest" (what is this?) outshines "aesthetic interest." The "People" pronounce judgment on literature, he says—although in fact it is the academics he despised who finally determine an author's status in the canon—and even novelists who write for money (i.e. to please the People) would be all right "if they wrote the Truth" (*Frank Norris: Novels and Essays* 1210). Norris is never sure whether the mass of People can be trusted or not, but by mentioning the "Truth" he solves his dilemma, since this is what he professes to be his own goal. In "The True Reward of the Novelist" he says sourly that the "businessmen"-writers are catering to "the taste of serving-men, the literature of chambermaids" (*Frank Norris: Novels and Essays* 1148); but then he makes his remarks that this same lower caste of "People" are the true judges of art. Most revealing is the wish, in "Novelists of the Future," to imitate his father's standards while obeying his mother's wishes. It is in this essay, the same one which presents the literary muse as a sort of tough, back-slapping Moran, that he calls novel-writing "virile" because you must go out into life to find your material. But it has already been shown here that stories told by others, and not raw "life," were Norris's main source-matter. What this mass of contradictions adds up to is a wish to prove that as an artist, the jeweler's son was performing a commercial act just as genuine as the one he had rejected in youth.

It is the same life-v.-literature question that the author always struggled with. By identifying authorship with profit-making, Norris hoped to show that literature could be part of what many people, ignoring the very fact that writers must earn a living, call in opposition the "real world." Hochman tells us that the persistent story-telling in his novels (for example, Maria Macapa's endlessly-repeated tale of family gold in *McTeague*) dramatizes this same aspect of "literature," the use of words as a shield against real experience, that Norris condemned (24-5). Norris's echoing of the Naturalistic doctrine that there is no imagination, only observation of real events, connects with his stated choice of action (or feeling) over thinking. Dillingham writes that this belief in self-control and accuracy of detail also stems from the author's painting days (*Frank Norris: Instinct and Art* 18). But Norris goes back further than this, to childhood and his belief in a "little dead story-teller" in one essay. In most adults, he believes, this story-teller is lost, but in those who still have a "sense of fiction," he is alive. This sort of gifted writer is described in words which delineate the familiar struggle once again: "He does not *know* [i.e. think], he *feels*" ("Story-Tellers vs. Novelists," *Frank Norris: Novels and Essays* 1192-4). The reader's quick reaction is to assume that Norris thinks of *himself* as a writer whose childhood delight in stories is still alive (certainly enough readers have found him childish!)—but does he? The sense of regret in his presentation of this "little dead" creature, plus his own frequent use of intellect (research) rather than feeling in forming his novels, suggest that Norris is accusing his father, who was so furious at the continuance into adulthood of the lead-soldier tales Frank wrote for his brother, of killing the story-teller.

And so we have the contradictions in *Responsibilities of the Novelist*, caused by this sense of anger and yet apology as Norris tries to judge his profession. In the passages above, he is stating his conflict affectingly and well. It is when he strays into defining virility that he betrays the desperation of his feelings as Frank, Sr.'s son.

"We are all Anglo-Saxon enough to enjoy the sight of a fight," remarks this man who sought out fights on the late 19th century's battlefields—and he makes the remark in the context of defining romance ("The True Reward of the Novelist," *Frank Norris: Novels and Essays* 1149). Once again, the wish to seem masculine enough (which, to Norris, often simply meant violent enough) is mixed in with his feelings about writing. He does not want to be like Presley, who, when confronted with Vanamee's statement of the Norris creed—"But why write? Why not *live* in it?"—answers wanly that he "must compromise" (*The Octopus* 610). Presley's "loss of strength," like Corthell's exaggerated refinement, is a symbol of the female-ruled "literature" side of the dialectic to which Norris fears he has surrendered. Pizer is right to say that in choosing Jadwin over Corthell at the end of *The Pit*, Laura is choosing life over art (*The Novels of Frank Norris* 172); but after reading Laura's story, we must wonder why the forceful, often insensitive Jadwin is finally presented as the right man for her, when Corthell is so much more like her. But Norris was never able to decide whether to reject the gentility of his upbringing; as Johnson succinctly puts it, "he yearned for both the pince-nez and the cow pony" ("The Frontier Behind Frank Norris's *McTeague*" 97). Even in the simplistic *Moran*, where he solves this dilemma by turning Ross Wilbur from a dandy to a brute, Norris as narrator shows this ambivalence when commenting on Wilbur's manly-life-at-sea plans—phrases like "so he told himself, so he believed" and "Wilbur honestly believed that" keep appearing (271-2). And in *The Pit*, a more mature work, he fails to solve the problem altogether.

Several critics (French, Ziff) feel that *The Pit* is successful because Norris was writing here about his own class, about what he knew best. But Norris was always writing from experience; the difference is simply that his last novel, and perhaps *Vandover*, seem more controlled and plausible because he is telling of this experience in familiar, rather than inflated and fanciful, terms. There is a realism to *The Pit*, despite the attempts to romanticize Jadwin, which puts the author a step closer to Henry James than to Jack London, and in fact James was aware of the book's existence. The archetypal wheat never clearly emerges from this novel's pages, as several critics have observed, and the narrator's comments on its power thus seem more inflated than in *The Octopus*. What emphasizes itself instead is the author's shifting emotions toward his parents.

Like S. Behrman, Jadwin challenges the wheat and is buried (metaphorically in this case) by it; but the more plausibly dramatized challenge here is that of the artist, Corthell, against the great capitalist's hold on his own wife. The similar roles of Norris's alter-ego artist characters have already been pointed out; but there is a forcefulness to Corthell's pursuit of Laura that contrasts him with the weak earlier artists, Vandover and Presley.

Presley, whom Richard Chase calls a part of Norris's personality that he escaped (196), can't understand force; his confusion makes him change beliefs constantly as he speaks to Caraher, then Shelgrim, then Vanamee. His role as a poet reminds us of Norris's derivative early work, *Yvernelle*, which he moved beyond thanks to Gates and other influences; perhaps, as Don Graham writes, Norris felt a novelist like himself would be less effeminate than an epic poet (100). Graham calls Presley an "anti-Norris." Vandover's immaturity and lack of depth show, even more, a character that the author may have been trying to escape by removing him firmly onto paper.

Corthell is similar, yet different. His connection to Norris's idle-rich Prufrockish side has already been pointed out. "Patrician," "Continental," "bohemian"—all of these adjectives used by Walker to describe Norris in youth (61) could describe this cultured, Europhile artist as well. Norris has two minds toward attention to dress; in *Moran*, whose Wilbur character he finds both silly and akin to himself, there is a motif of changes in clothing that represent changes in character. The dandified Wilbur is "born again" when Captain Kitchell first forces him to change to sailor's clothes, and the "only traces of his former self," in the narrator's words, are not a personality trait but his boots (19). Further south, his dress alters again to "a suit of jeans and wicker sandals, such as the coolies wore," at just the point when he is gaining the respect of the force-wielder, the Captain (44-5).

Corthell never changes clothes, but he is also in contact with the "force" represented by the author's father—not simply from stumbling into violent situations, like Wilbur or like Presley at the ranchers' battle (Annixter even says to him there, "Best keep out of this, Pres") (*The Octopus* 981), but by wielding force himself. He asks Laura to marry him before Jadwin does, but the incessant attentions of the businessman (reminding one more of a pestering child than a strong suitor) lead her to yield. After her marriage, Corthell returns from Europe and courts her with methods as various, and successful, as talking about the God-in-nature transcendentalism Norris himself believed in and playing the organ with his "long, slim hands" until she drinks in "the very essence of passion, the voluptuousness that is a veritable anguish" (*The Pit* 237-8). When Jadwin bursts in on this scene, crowing about making more money and turning on all the lights in an obvious contrast to Corthell's stained-glass dimness, he seems boorish and unattractive compared to the sensual artist.

In fact, Jadwin, like the somewhat similar father-figure Bennett (and unlike McTeague with his "sewer" of desire) seems a husband in name but not in conjugal passion. Corthell, by contrast, is a man with normal sexual desires. A similar contrast occurs in *Vandover and the Brute*, in which another of its "good" characters, the cross-named man Dolly Haight, shows us the uncertainty Norris felt about a man's physical role. Like Turner, Dolly is not just virtuous but seemingly asexual. He seems as prudish as the narrator when with his male friends, speaking angrily at length about a woman who got drunk and commenting on Vandover's attraction to a "fast" woman: "Why *can't* a fellow keep straight when there are such a lot of *nice* girls?" (69). (Geary's more direct comment on the same page is, "Cheap meat!") More revealingly, when he proposes to Turner, Haight presents marriage as a motherly or sisterly relationship rather than a sexual-partner one. He cannot even say the word "wife" in his final sentence: "You have already influenced me as a mother or sister should have done; what if I should ask you to be—to be the *other* to me, the one that's best of all?" (62-3). One critic is alarmed that a woman one wants to sleep with should be compared to a close relative (Cooperman, "Frank Norris and the Werewolf of Guilt" 257), and Norris seems uncertain about Haight, too. He gives him the name of a child's toy, and ends his part in the novel with a schoolboy-myth fate: he gets V.D. because the prostitute Flossie kisses him on a cut lip. This seems less another example of the author's cruel-chance motif, and more another of the book's punishments—perhaps a man should not be *either* too pure or too sensual. "Couldn't avoid sex after all, Dolly!" we can almost hear the author laughing as he writes this scene.

And he is tempted to punish his father-figure in *The Pit* for the same avoidance. In fact, Laura may even commit adultery. Years before, Corthell had left the scene and allowed Jadwin to capture Laura, but now, obsessed by his speculating passion, the businessman himself exits. "Let that Mr. Corthell take my place," he says to his wife—at a theatre outing he can't attend, he means, but the line of course foreshadows more (270). Another day, after Jadwin again breaks a date, the artist is there to croon to Laura, "What, you are all alone?" (277). She lets him kiss her hand, and he produces the heart-shaped, red-stained, sulphur-smelling matchbox that Joseph Katz, in an article detailing hidden eroticism in the novels of Norris's time, asserts is a symbol of sexual intercourse to come (48). And immediately after describing the matchbox, Norris's narrator adds a simple sentence: "An hour later Corthell left her" (*The Pit* 284). Is Katz right? Corthell's line at a later meeting, "I should not have believed that I was strong enough to trust myself" (291), suggests so, but we can't be certain that Norris actually went so far as to sexually couple characters inspired by his mother and himself.

In this latter scene, Laura tries to tell Corthell that they can't meet any more, but he responds with an act Jadwin is never seen to do: the standard romantic-hero conquest of his lover with a powerful kiss. She feels "a wild bound of the heart," and he extracts a promise to see her once more (292). And yet, Laura's husband, whose last name suggests that he'll always "win," does win. For when Corthell comes to take her away, he stupidly decides that they'll wait until tomorrow to elope, though her husband is nowhere to be seen. Off goes Corthell, on comes Jadwin—"My husband, my husband!" cries Laura (394)—and a marital reconciliation that critics have rightly called somewhat preposterous ends the novel.

Is this sudden shift in a story that appears ready to lead toward Laura's running off with the artist what Lynn says it is?—that is, "the artist had lost out to the businessman, the father had beaten the son, once and for all time" (207). This is an easy Oedipal conclusion to draw, but there are other possible interpretations. For one thing, Jadwin does not beat anyone by regaining Laura, for he doesn't master her in the end (as at first)—he has been crushed, financially and in spirit, by his wheat corner's failure, and like Bennett, thus wins his woman only when he loses some of his masculine strength. Ziff thinks Norris finally makes Corthell more attractive, and Jadwin in the end is acceptable only as "a broken man" (272). But this is not the right phrase to use about either this novel or *A Man's Woman*. Norris's wish to unite masculine and feminine, denied in the early novels when men like Vandover refuse the help of their "good women," is fulfilled in his last three books. Corthell belongs only to the "literature" side, and Jadwin and Bennett, initially, only to the "life" side; but it is the transcendence of opposites, the achievement of nirvana, that Norris prizes. The end of *The Pit* hints, less obviously than that of *The Octopus* and perhaps less clearly, that this achievement is possible.

There is one more answer. One could claim, as Geismar does, that Norris simply wanted an ending that would fulfill his audience's moral code (44)—in short, give them a conventional "happy ending." But isn't there someone else who would prefer this happy ending, despite the seeming irreconcilable differences in the personalities of the fictional, as well as the real, couple? That someone, of course, is Frank Norris. The author himself, reversing in fiction what he could not control in life, kept the Jadwins together.

Fathers and Sons in the Novels

At one point in *The Octopus*, there is a sudden focus on one animal that Presley passes in his wanderings through the valley of wheat: "the monarch, the king, the great Durham bull, maintaining his lonely state, unapproachable, austere" (875). And in the Big Dipper mine scene in *McTeague*, a completely different character appears just as fleetingly—a slight man with prematurely grey hair (531). The latter is, in one of his typical insider jokes of the early novels, Frank Norris himself. These figures—the powerful beast-father, master of procreation, and the uncertainly rebellious son—are repeated over and over in Norris's fiction as his two basic representatives of the male gender.

Fathers and sons appear more often in these books than successfully-breeding mothers do; *The Octopus*, with Magnus and his two sons, one loyal and one traitorous (reminding us of the battling impulses of Norris himself), is the novel in which this relationship is most central, but it occurs elsewhere as well. Vandover's guilt-ridden relationship with his own "unapproachable, austere" father, McTeague's Zolaesque inheritance from his bestial sire, and the wrecked families of the Dykes and Hoovens in *The Octopus*, will all be examined here; but so will the towering father-like characters already often mentioned, the forceful businessmen without sons, the seemingly gelded Durham bulls.

As noted, the Norris of the "silver spoon" days, the erring son whose father hadn't yet run out of patience with him (or his mother), was not the Norris who wrote his only significant works, the novels. It was not until after his parents' initial separation in 1892, and especially their divorce and his disowning two years later, that Frank, Jr. began to write something beyond the childishly violent short stories and plodding poetry. Had the parental battle continued longer, this Californian Peter Pan who never finished anything would probably have written nothing worth remembering—just superficial attempts, in scarlet adventure tales like *Moran*, to manage his discomfiting middle position in the brute-v.-refinement struggle. Instead he was forced to grow up, and thus produced novels which illuminate for us today the national conflicts of a hundred years ago.

The first two, written practically together during the year after the divorce, were *Vandover and the Brute* and *McTeague*. (The second is viewed as the later work simply because it was not finished until the author's nature-sabbatical in 1897.) Norris's fear of, or wish for, punishment, rather than any truly naturalistic character-decay idea, is the true theme of *Vandover*. Van is without a mother for the entire book (a fact to be stressed more in Chapter Four here), and without a father for much of it; and as Hochman writes, these losses, not some bestial drive toward sex, are what affect him most. He is "perpetually afraid of encountering an unexpected blow" and feels responsible for all of his misfortunes. Yet the narrator, instead of understanding these feelings or even taking note of the losses' significance, supports the hero's own guilty view (Hochman 46, 48).

Who is *Vandover*'s narrator? There is more in the voice than mere condemnation, as in the recognition, after his father's death, of "a crying need to be loved as his father had loved him" (117). (Or his mother?) But shortly afterward, when Van seems to have recovered from this loss and falls into indolence again, this more characteristic intrusive passage appears: "But Vandover made another fatal mistake: the brute in him had only been stunned; the snake was only soothed" (132). The Satanic-phallic snake symbol is obvious, and the word "brute," as in the similar passages in *McTeague*, is typical. It seems that the moral tract-writer whom French sees in Norris, the stern voice of the 19th century, is rampant here. Even Vandover's inability to go hungry to save money after he becomes poor is a crime to this narrator: "the evil, hideous brute ... demanded to be fed" (239).

The answer is that this voice is not lecturing the audience, as a tract-writer does, but the character—or more precisely, the aspects of the character represented by the same author who writes these words. Or is it the author? More likely, the God who has turned away rather than never existed in this novel, the God whose eye looms over *The Octopus* and whose power is incarnate in Vandover's rich father, is pointing his huge finger accusingly down at this weak, malleable, trembling young man. Norris is assuming the character not of himself, but of the father he failed to satisfy, when he writes these passages.

Vandover's own father is called "the Governor," as is Magnus Derrick. Other than that, he has no known name—perhaps he's the universal strong father who "governs" all. The first thing Norris tells us about him, showing his familiar ambivalence about commerce in doing so, is that he's bored and crippled by being unable to enjoy anything but business (5). The only thing this businessman-father does to guide his son is trick him into studying the encyclopedia by claiming a dollar was lost somewhere among its pages. The child Vandover is something of an actor as well as an artist: "For days he would pretend to be some dreadful sort of character, he did not know whom, talking to himself, stamping and shaking his fists; then he would dress himself in an old smoking-cap, a red table-cloth and one of his father's discarded Templar swords, and pose before the long mirrors ranting and scowling" (9). The "dreadful sort of character," of course, is his father; Van is burlesqueing the only role-model he can find.

Vandover's father-centered guilt at discovering vice has been mentioned; although one or two critics have written that he is rebelling against his father here, his exaggerated sense of shame betrays a weak, doomed rebellion at best. Meanwhile, he pursues art, encouraged by the "Old Gentleman" with his little gifts of money; the art v. commerce battle arises again here, for the just-disinherited Norris must have known that Vandover could never have lived his indolent life of painting practice and male-bonding evenings at the Imperial without his rich sire's backing. In fact, the Governor seems to know little about the son whose vices and vague ambitions he supports. When Van confesses to him that Ida Wade committed suicide because he made her pregnant, he is stunned, having expected the confession to be some simple boy's problem—"but this was the crime of a man" (80). Instead of offering, as an involved God would, either punishment or absolution, he can't handle the situation and simply tells Van to leave the room.

There is little sense of Norris's admiration of Shelgrim-like giants here; only a distant deity who, like the father the author himself had lost, offers no support or even opposition. Vandover feels little toward him except his most familiar emotion, guilt; though Maxwell Geismar creates a complex for him, writing that "a complete father fixation had concealed and repressed the incestuous drives" for his mother, there is no real evidence of either (60). Geismar *is* right in noting that Van is a sexual being only before his father's death; afterward his central vice is gambling. Perhaps without a wielder of the male libido-sword to follow—or, however weakly, to rebel against—the son is no longer drawn to the world of women. (Or perhaps the Ida Wade incident just soured him on sexual conquest.)

The absence of a mother always has its impact on Van too, of course. French, seeing what some other critics have, defines the character's problem as a lack of depth and inability to cope rather than an addiction to vice: "Van's trouble is not that he degenerates, but that he fails to grow" (59). This reminds us of Freud's belief that a person whose infantile needs are not fulfilled remains an infant. In his need for feminine influence, the Governor's son is himself often given the adjective "feminine," and this description of him after coming out of the bath and learning of Ida's death could almost be of a woman: "his long white arms agitated and shaking, his wet and shining hair streaming far over his face" (*Vandover and the Brute* 78).

Then, when he goes to his father for help, the need to transcend the purely masculine side of life reaches its peak. His father returns, seeming (by being silent) to forgive him—but now his son no longer wants a God-the-Father. Instead we have this significant sentence: "'Oh, governor!' he cried. It was as if it had been a mother or a dear sister" (82). For his few remaining pages in the book Vandover's father seems a kind figure, no longer distant but no longer really male; he is last seen daintily waving a handkerchief in farewell as Van sails off on his fateful ship voyage.

And so, as soon as Van's father becomes a fit replacement for his mother, the punishing author removes him, too. Vandover survives the shipwreck only to find his father dead upon returning home. It is impossible to ignore the timing of this novel's writing when we read of how the son feels like a criminal going into his father's iron box of precious possessions, although he is his rightful heir; or when we read the sentimental but effective description of Vandover after the funeral. "His grief came over him again keener than ever and he put his arms clumsily about the old hat, weeping and whispering to himself: 'Oh, my poor, dear old dad—I'm never going to see you again, never, never! Oh, my dear, kind old governor!'" (115-6). For Frank Norris never saw his father again, either.

Without either parent, the adult who had already impregnated a woman becomes, as noted, a child again. Several critics have made the point that he is like a "good boy" in the last scene, working hard and accepting a small monetary reward from the father (naturally) of the family whose house he cleans. The boy who watches him work is compared by Hochman to the "wide-eyed little boy" Van himself was, seeing his mother die in the first scene (54). But they are not really equal, for one simple reason. "*There* was a smart little boy for you," his parents think when he shouts at Vandover. "Ah, he'd be a man before his mother" (*Vandover and the Brute* 259). Of course, Vandover has no mother, and never really becomes a man.

Norris's anger toward this character is shown by his relationship to his other Harvard-year hero, McTeague. Both are negatively affected by their fathers, but neither is treated with much sympathy. Van is the upper-class version of McTeague—as Hart puts it, "they are equally incapable of coping with life" (*A Novelist in the Making* 42)—but Norris does not show any greater respect for the character closer to himself. A passage like this one early in *Vandover*, echoing with derisive laughter, shows the opposite: "He prayed that he might be a good boy and live a long time and go to Heaven when he died and see his mother; that the next Saturday might be sunny all day long, and that the end of the world might not come while he was alive" (7).

McTeague is never seen to pray, but he would certainly share Van's wish for sunny days off, as the novel's famous first scene detailing his Sunday idleness shows. Like his upper-class counterpart (or his counterpart in force, Bennett, for that matter), he is practically untouched by feminine influence when his novel begins. Unlike Bennett, he is a Norris "superman" only in a physical sense—"immensely strong, stupid, docile, obedient" (*McTeague* 264)—and the author celebrates his stupidity in the novel at least as much as his strength. What hands molded this creature? Norris's attempts to use heredity as a plot element appear in many short stories, but only here among the novels. The influence of McTeague's parents is described on the very first page, and is as much as part of the character's introduction as his concertina and his love of warmth and beer. His father, the "irresponsible animal ... a brute, crazy with alcohol," and his mother, an "overworked drudge" who cooked for the miners (263), are his Zolaesque foundation.

Both are quickly dispensed with, as quickly as Vandover's mother, but their importance is shown by the emphasis of critics on not only the father's bestiality, but the mother's prodding ambition. Freedman writes in his article that they "represent, respectively, society and instinct, outer and inner" (55)— but in the opposite order to Jung's archetypes. The cook (and thus feeder, as Freedman notes, like any Great Mother) is the society-force, the superego, the only reason McTeague becomes a dentist, while the drunken father is pure id.

Father-surrogates are more important in *McTeague* than actual fathers—a role McTeague himself never achieves. The only father we really meet in the novel is Trina's, the laughable Teutonic cliche, Mr. Sieppe. A grotesque version of the strong fathers we meet elsewhere in Norris's novels, he is constantly described as military, as when controlling his family's movements on the picnic McTeague attends with Trina and her family. The pathetic son August—who, like Blix, has his narrative-voice name changed by what other characters call him, in this case a dialect-mangled "Owgooste"— has a toy boat both he and his father would like to sail in a pond. "'No, no!' wailed August. 'I want to play with ut.' 'Obey!' thundered Mr. Sieppe. August subsided" (314). And the imperious father promptly sinks the boat.

In the Sieppes' first move, to Los Angeles after Trina marries, the father is compared to Napoleon and the move he organizes to an army maneuvre. It is the same language Norris will use later about Jadwin and his pit, but here, shortly after losing his father, he chooses to laugh rather than salute. In the end, after money troubles, the family moves to New Zealand— Glen A. Love's "inept urbanites" giving up the struggle to survive in the harsh urban world.

It is the surrogate fathers, those who have no children but play the Godlike roles of rewarder and punisher, that wield the real strength in this novel. One is Trina's rich Uncle Oelbermann, with whom she first invests her money. He is treated as a master figure by the family, and when he speaks his only words after the wedding—that most labored of marital cliches, "You have not lost a daughter, but have gained a son"—everyone listens in a hush and is "profoundly impressed" (386). But like Vandover's father, he is too distant and silent to help in the characters' lives. When Trina keeps drawing on her invested money, after McTeague has become brutal to her and the lust for gold is her only pleasure, her uncle, the "great man," does not ask why but simply gets annoyed and tells her to take it all.

It is Marcus Schouler, McTeague's rival throughout the book, who is finally the true male (Death Valley is the female) punisher. Freedman calls Marcus a father-figure, who breaks McTeague's pipe (his pacifier) and is a better devourer even than the dentist, putting an entire billiard ball in his mouth (58). (Perhaps his ability to do this, while McTeague almost chokes trying the same trick, symbolizes the effect of taking a woman, as McTeague is about to do, into one's life.) Though Marcus awards Trina to his neighbor, like God bestowing a mate on Adam (and as if she has no voice in the matter herself), he later sees her, as Zerkow does Maria, only in terms of wealth: "If it hadn't been for me ... you wouldn't have had a cent of [her winnings]—no, not a cent. Where's my share, I'd like to know?" (363). Yet he later protects Maria when her husband first threatens her life, and finally causes McTeague's death in vengeance for Trina's murder. George Spangler, in an article exploring the sexual themes in the novel, says Marcus "represents in Freudian terms the father who punishes for the incestuous wishes underlying castration anxiety" (56). The latter complexes seem no more appropriate to *McTeague* than to *Vandover* (McTeague has no living relatives to feel incestuous wishes for), but there is no question about the punishment.

And so McTeague dies in the desert, and his creator moves on, in his later novels, to characters he respects more, and makes less illustrative of his conflicts and more of the solutions he desires to those conflicts.

Moran of the Lady Letty, ostensibly about love between a man and a woman, is really about a man (or a near-boy) finding the father-figure he needs to teach him true, brutal masculinity. In keeping with Norris's wish for a "rta" or "tian"-filled being who can represent both sides of his struggle, that figure is not a man, but a woman who *is* a man in all but physique. This book was written between the author's two attempts to assert his own masculinity in the most traditional arena, and thus is very different from *A Man's Woman* and the wheat novels, which were written after both of those attempts had failed.

This may be the only novel in which Norris deserves the negative critical reaction he has received over a hundred years. All of his worst features in plot-creation, if not in style—the delight in blood, the racism, the adherence to popular ideas of evolution and bestiality that he barely understood, the inability to create convincing female characters—rage through this implausible sea-yarn. But a careful look beneath the plot suggests ambivalence toward naturalism, the adventure-story genre, and even the definition of manliness by violence. Larzer Ziff says of *Moran* that "Norris knew better than that" (266). Perhaps the novel's subtext shows that he did.

It has been noted that Norris here wrote a generic adventure story to make money, just as Condy was advised to do in *Blix*—and that like Condy, he wrote it with "Captain Jack" Hodgson, himself a combination of father-image and adventure-cliche when he appears in both novels. But as Joseph McElrath points out, he was showing his negative feelings about venal writing in this book just as much as in *The Responsibilities of the Novelist*. McElrath sees Norris's authorial hand behind the absurdity of Moran's "might-makes-right" Darwinism—Hoang, the bestial Chinaman whom the narrator nonetheless notes is honest, becomes a villain in the plot only after Moran breaks her agreement with him. Moran begs the moral question, i.e. she deserves the profit from her sea-plunder because she does, just like Captain Kitchell before her. To McElrath, this may be satirical, with Norris's personal attitude not conforming to his narrative voice ("The Erratic Design of Frank Norris's *Moran of the Lady Letty*" 116-7). "In short, the sometimes serious Norris occasionally seems to stand back and enjoy the ludicrous scenes that develop before his eyes" (118).

Norris may not have been quite so clever as this, but we've already seen in *Vandover* that his narrator was not always necessarily himself. In that novel, Norris has Geary repeat his Social Darwinism so often that it becomes hollow; but in *Moran*, when the heroine shouts such lines as, "Now the [sea loot] belongs to the strongest of us and I'm glad of it ... The strongest of us are going to live and the weakest are going to die," should we trust him as narrator when he says solemnly that this nonsense makes Wilbur "ashamed of himself and proud of her" (191-2)? Perhaps not. Norris's semi-sardonic view of Wilbur has already been noted. And this is shown even more in the descriptions of his self-justifying amnesia between Moran's naturalistic outburst and the actual fight. When she kidnaps Hoang, who has come only to negotiate, Wilbur can't remember anything but a "rush forward"; now they have "taken Hoang prisoner, whether by treachery or not Wilbur did not exactly know; and, even if unfair means had been used, he could not repress a feeling of delight and satisfaction" (195-6). Later, just before the fight, the brute-in-training can't recall why he is suddenly holding a knife (211). Clearly Norris, who McElrath points out is ironic even on the first page of *Moran*, knows Wilbur better than his young hero knows himself.

What this novel essentially tells, again, is the standard tale (seen in an earlier Robert Louis Stevenson novel and a later Jack London one) of an effeminate man taught toughness by a sea-captain—but with a strange gender-reversing twist appropriate to Norris. Its first one-third, before Captain Kitchell's death, is the standard part. We meet Ross Wilbur knowing nothing about him except his refined dress and manner and his movement in the California "set" from which Blix and Condy escape. (He has "plenty of jaw," but Norris will not use his favorite word for the jaws of his strong characters, "salient," here.) (6) Like Condy, this is a character whom Norris based partly on himself, yet gave no visible parents. Thus we can only guess that he is probably a fellow "silver spoon" sufferer, taught Lynn's "winner take all" Algerism from the same rich, Eastern-college background as Norris himself.

A more brutal and practical study of life is waiting for him. Thinking it'll be "amusing" to loaf around the San Francisco waterfront before an evening debutante-ball, he watches such things as grain ships with wheat harvests (again!) going off (7-8). Then a little man in a brown sweater—who is referred to afterward, in an early sign of this novel's clothes-as-character motif, only as "the brown sweater"—drugs Wilbur and hands him over to Captain Kitchell as a shanghaied seaman.

This character's parental status is constantly shown by the way he speaks to Wilbur. His first words of insult are, "It ain't ought to be let around loose without its ma," and he at first calls his new crewman "angel child"

(15-6). More interesting are the Captain's sarcastic references to fatherly love. Wilbur's sailor suit is "a present of and no charge, because he [i.e. I] loves you so"; and he will sleep beside him, because "son, I natch'ly love you" (18, 38). Norris could hardly be more obvious. Kitchell's father-figure role would be clear enough, as this "enormous man with a face like a setting moon" (a reversal of the usual symbol of male power, the sun) (14) holds sway over his younger captive and uses it in part to educate him—the second chapter is titled "A Nautical Education." But Wilbur's decision not to escape when a boat with his "set" comes close by, and the Captain's addressing him regularly as "sonny" and "son" after they leave San Francisco, underline it. The young dilettante wants to be "born again" and tutored by this forceful man, just as Norris may have sometimes wished at this point that he could step back and become his own father's apprentice.

Out on the ocean (which, like their boat the *Bertha Millner*, provides the initial female half of this new parentage), Wilbur and Kitchell become closer, for reasons which the surprisingly myopic narrator calls "vague." The absurd notion that a gentleman's training makes him superior anywhere is illustrated when they send out a smaller boat to catch a turtle. "'Kin you row, son?' asked Kitchell, with sudden suspicion. Wilbur smiled. 'I'm going to show you the Bob Cook stroke we used in our boat in '95, when we beat Harvard'" (49). (Kitchell is duly impressed.) The next thing sighted is a Norwegian boat with a distress signal flag, and here the might-makes-right greed-lesson which Moran later teaches first appears. It's not enough for the Captain to talk of plundering the boat; Norris has him proudly speak at length about what a "hog" (he spells the word out), "swine" and "shoat with both feet in the trough" he is (61). But what awaits Kitchell on the *Lady Letty* is not profit, but his own death and replacement by an even stronger "father."

Moran's father is dead on the boat, and his papers show that her mother died years ago (another Norris orphan). The first view of her is only of an arm, and then eyes. The Captain thinks it's a male sailor, and the narrator goes along with the illusion: "He was a tall, well-made fellow, with ruddy complexion and milk-blue eyes ... " But, when "his" breast swells, Wilbur says, "My God, it's a girl!" (68-9).

Wilbur wants to save this girl from the "hog" (he now thinks disapprovingly) Kitchell—and at the moment he's feeling most impotent against his "father," Mother Nature intervenes to protect Moran. The Captain is on the *Lady Letty*, stealing things and singing (appropriately, though he doesn't know it) a song about dropping down to Hell, when a tropical squall hits and he sinks with the ship. And as soon as the Biblical storm has done its work, it ceases "like the rolling up of a scroll" (93).

Who has been saved by this deified ally? Not the usual heroine: "She was not pretty ... and her skeleton was too massive ... Her hands were red and hard, and even beneath the coarse sleeve of the oilskin coat one could infer that the biceps and deltoids were large and powerful. She was coarse-fibred, no doubt, mentally as well as physically" (71-2). And though Wilbur is still not a total brute, having felt "sick to vomiting" when Kitchell threw Moran's father to the sharks (86), the storm suddenly awakens this creature. Kitchell's replacement, who will teach Wilbur to act in properly bloody fashion. "Are you going to drown like rats on a plank?" she shouts, "savage, splendid, dominant," and gives instructions that save the *Bertha Millner* in nautical talk that could just as well have been the Captain's (90). She not only takes over as captain, but wears some of Kitchell's clothing the next day—and in this book, clothing is identity.

Lynn compares Moran's spirit to that of Norris's father (182), and this seems apt in light of her role in the novel. Completely unbelievable as a lover, despite Wilbur's absurd lines like, "I think you're a ripping fine girl ... by jingo, you're—you're splendid" (*Moran of the Lady Letty* 101), she is entirely appropriate as a Bennett-like paternal master of force. (Her only quasi-sexual feature is her hair, massive and striking like that of Trina and Lloyd.) Her contact with libido, the energy of the universe, is shown not only by her body and character and "her" storm, but by the appearance of the *Lady Letty*, with sharks swimming around it, and a "reek of coal gas" and terrible heat on board (66), it is practically Hell—a hell which claims Kitchell amid his song, so that the even more demonic Moran can replace him. Her role as a "father" is underlined by her odd, upside-down relationship to her own father, whom she never mourns. As mentioned before, it is the father who represents the literature side here, with his cabin full of books that Moran won't read; and in an obvious contrast, the captain's room of the *Lady Letty* is described as "dainty" and "charming" (75). Only once does Moran speak of her father afterward, calling him by his unimpressive first name, Eilert, and saying that now she has "not a tie, not a relative, not even a friend, and I don't wish it" (171).

Of course "rta"—divine force, the wheat in *The Octopus*—has no friends, being far above such things. Moran is libido, "the primordial creative principle" (Jung 5:138) personified, but with any sexual aspect erased. Divine force has no lovers either, so nothing is more laughable in this laughable book than Norris's attempt to mate Moran and Wilbur. Even after Wilbur declares his love, she is described in a passage that seems to describe a man—weapon, "muscular neck," "massive jaw" (172)—and they sleep side by side on the beach, but the young man resists his natural impulses. What makes her his true "mate," then? During the fight with the Chinamen she, "blind to friend or foe ... deaf to reason," goes wild and attacks *him*; and Wilbur, who has just killed his first man, meets this "impersonal force that it was incumbent upon him to conquer"—which is in fact the woman he supposedly loves—in battle (217-8). In a truly bizarre scene, the man and woman fight for four pages until he punches her senseless.

If we see Moran as a real woman, then this scene is totally offensive. And unfortunately, when we recall Norris's enjoyment of being "master" over his wife, such a view is partially correct. But the roles of the novel's three main characters are such that another view is correct, too. The ideal student bests his own teacher, and just as Moran replaced Kitchell as ruling brute, Wilbur now replaces her. "A Change in Leaders" is the name of the chapter following the battle; and in it, she not only declares that she loves him, but unaccountably becomes tender and concerned for a wounded Chinese crewman, while Wilbur adopts her old amoral "only the strong survive" creed. All descriptions of activity on board now begin "Wilbur allowed," "Wilbur had the hands," etc.—and this is also where the young gentleman gives Hoang his speech about not challenging white people.

Of course, Moran must die after such a degradation—she is no longer herself. When Hoang kills her, it is more than a simple murder; it is all of Norris's ambivalence about gender uniting in one scene of confused condemnation of a woman who has adopted only the female half of his dialectic. "Only a few weeks ago, and she would have fought with Hoang without hesitation and without mercy ... But she had learned since to know what it meant to be dependent; to rely for protection upon some one who was stronger than she; to know her weakness; to know that she was at last a woman, and to be proud of it" (284). Proud?—the Frank Norris whose mother tried to condemn *him* to dependency on the womanly "literature" side of life will not tolerate that! As she cries out for Wilbur, the inferior-race villain stabs her to death.

Whether Norris was partly ironic when writing this blood-and-thunder epic, or whether the book is simply so weird that one must hope he's being ironic, he never wrote anything like it again. By now, most of the events described in *Blix* had already happened, and in killing Moran—in making Wilbur the final inheritor of the paternal role—he may have been celebrating his own new status as adult, prospective husband, potential father. From here on, the early novels' "red-blooded" delight in violence and racial-superiority themes is gone (except for some resurgence in *The Octopus*), and, starting with the story of his own courtship, Norris focuses on the theme of genuine love.

Vandover failed partly because his prospective "man's woman," Turner Ravis, failed; now that character, with her name squeezed (as Geismar first noticed) into Travis Bessemer's first name, becomes Norris's first true "man's woman," Blix. (Condy starts calling Turner "Blix" during the novel, and as with August/Owgooste, she then has this name in the narrative voice as well.) This story is much more one of Condy's finding a mother-figure to replace his own invisible mother than one of fathers and sons, so there is little to say about it here. Travis's "self-centered," mumbling father, whom Norris calls "one of those men who seem entirely disassociated from their families" and almost without "paternal spirit or instincts" (*Blix* 106), is a character who reminds us again of Norris's own father's absence; but he is like this mainly to give the heroine a chance to show her mothering abilities toward her younger siblings, and toward him as well. Condy has no father.

Only in Captain Jack, a figure who helps *Moran* segue into this very different book, is there a sign of the paternal strength seen in other novels. In *Moran* he appears briefly at the end, as Captain Hodgson (the real man's name), to tell Wilbur that he has found the dying Moran on the boat. In *Blix* his surname is Hoskins. He "had been everywhere, had seen everything, and had done most of the things worth doing," including travelling in the Arctic and captaining nasty Chinamen—so he has a hand in all three middle novels (217). It's hinted that he is in California hiding from the law. "If you hate a man," he says—as Condy, entranced by this character, starts imagining the fictionalized version of *Moran* he will write with him—"you lay awake nights biting your mattress, just thinking how you hate him; an' if you love a woman, good Lord, how you do *love* her!" (222). Clearly he knows the close link between the two instincts that dominates Norris's novels.

And in fact, strangely enough, Captain Jack's main role in the story is to meet through Condy and Blix's manipulations, and then suddenly marry, a woman probably inspired by Norris's mother. Why does the author pair two such characters—one a prim lover of poetry, with Gertrude Doggett's stage experience, and the other a two-dimensional refugee from a sea chanty who all but sports a parrot on his shoulder? (The contrived marriage is likely to fail, anyway, as Captain Jack says near the novel's end that he's "got to schemin' again"—or in other words, is likely to desert his wife to pursue more half-criminal sea adventures.) (269) Perhaps it is a humorous subplot echo of what the main plot of *Blix* is: a declaration of independence not only from Norris's mother, but from both of his parents. "K.D.B." is partly a cartoon version of Gertrude; and Captain Jack, compared to Frank Norris, Sr., is an even more rejecting image. The Sunday-school-teaching businessman has been shoved aside by a proudly amoral character who represents nothing more nor less than a boy's-novel quintessence of masculinity.

In *A Man's Woman*, the laughter ends and Norris begins to paint his portrait of the true hero. Although usually labelled as bad, this book—despite its weakness of belabored analysis of which the author himself was aware—has an important place in the development of his themes. Its exploration of the seesawing between compromise and conflict in a love-relationship is more thorough and realistic than in any other Norris novel; and if it had not been written, its far more praised successor, *The Octopus*, probably would not have been the book it is.

At first the novel seems to be only about what Jay Martin called the "romance of force." Its hero, Bennett, is seen fighting the forces of nature, personified as the Enemy and the also-capitalized Ice, with all the power of will a Norris man can have. When we remember that Norris likes the strength in a "salient" lower face—even his best women have it, Blix with a salient chin (*Blix* 108) and Lloyd whose "chin was not small" (*A Man's Woman* 42)— we can hardly miss this point in the description of Bennett. "His lower jaw was huge almost to deformity, like that of the bulldog, the chin salient, the mouth close-gripped, with great lips, indomitable, brutal" (2). Determined to make his man ugly (and he uses the word), Norris even gives him a cast in one eye. Yet this is no McTeague-like brute; he is looking "thoughtfully" out at the ice in this first scene, and his journal, an intellectual product, is already being quoted (3).

His actions as the story unfolds also progress upward from simple brutality. When fighting the Enemy (itself another form of the Great Mother, as we will see in Chapter Four), he is the dragon-father in all its pitiless strength. No action is too hideous to ensure survival; dogs are shot and fed to both the other dogs and the men, and one man who falls crippled is left behind. Yet Bennett also kicks the will to live back into Adler when he wants to give up and die, and he is seen reading a prayer book over the grave of the expedition's first casualty. And though he is almost as big as Shelgrim in his wielding of the paternal sword—"On that vast frame of bone and muscle fatigue seemed to leave no trace. Upon that inexorable bestial determination difficulties beyond belief left no mark ... that indomitable man of iron whom no fortune could break nor bend, and who imposed his will upon them as if it were a yoke of steel" (11, 19)—his tempering into a hero who also accepts the feminine side is already being telegraphed. At one point he has a Geary-like thought when tempted to abandon his men—"He, the strongest, the fittest, would survive. Was it not right that the mightiest should live? Was it not the great law of nature?" (38)—but refuses to yield to it. (Perhaps this is also the self-declared end to Norris's efforts at naturalism.) And he mentions Lloyd Searight (her last name a reminder of her more simplistic predecessor, Moran), his loved one, in an early conversation with Ferriss.

Five years had passed now since Frank Norris lost his father. He was on the verge of his own marriage. Both of his experiments with war had ended, the second in total disillusionment about its violence. Having already wounded the dragon, by making the "son" replace two "fathers" in *Moran* and trivializing the father-figure in *Blix*, it is no surprise that now he should complete its slaughter. Bennett's taming by the feminine element is more subtle than McTeague's destruction after a woman enters his little world of animal comforts, and so some critics have missed it. Donald Pizer was the first to notice that Norris was not simply celebrating his hero's "superman" status here, but demonstrating "that a Bennett can become the victim of his iron resolve ... Bennett's career in the Arctic had conditioned him to respond to all opposition as forces to be subdued." Brute force isn't enough; selfishness and pride must be overcome (*The Novels of Frank Norris* 105-6). And George Johnson, who sees Bennett as an intelligent McTeague, says he's "socialized and purified by feminine idealism" ("Frank Norris and Romance" 61).

When Bennett learns that Lloyd is taking on a typhoid case which already killed one nurse, Norris starts chiding his character's response at once.

He thinks "with blind, unreasoning directness" that Lloyd is in danger; he chooses "instantly to believe that Lloyd was near her death, and once the idea was fixed in his brain it was not thereafter to be reasoned away" (*A Man's Woman* 102). Lloyd, for her part, has faced the same "Enemy" and is proud of her profession and her willingness to wrestle with death, unlike a nurse transparently named Harriet Freeze who avoided an infectious case. Freeze's action is described in war language, "cowardice in the presence of the Enemy"—and in case we've missed these words, Norris then tells us of the "esprit de corps" of Lloyd's group of nurses in "battle with disease" (44). In other words, she is as masculine as Bennett in some ways (though not as masculine perhaps as Moran!), and so his wish to save her from this "foolish, mistaken notion of duty" (102)—a notion no different from his own in the Arctic—shows both misunderstanding and disrespect of her. Lloyd may be the ideal "man's woman," but Norris tells us in the simplest terms that his flawed hero has not learned to transcend the dialectic. "Bennett was not a woman's man" (103).

Now begins the interminable scene that has annoyed many readers—twenty-one pages of Bennett and Lloyd arguing outside Ferriss's door about whether the nurse should abandon her patient. This chapter would also be of wearying length if the entire scene were analyzed here. One line can serve to show how desperate Norris was to make his point: "If he was determined, she was obstinate; if he was resolved, she was stubborn; if he was powerful, she was unyielding" (116-7). Bennett is not on his own ground here, however, as shown by Lloyd's dignified words of anger and her line, "We are not in Kolyuchin Bay [Siberia], Mr. Bennett" (118). Kolyuchin Bay, like the "Magdalena Bay" of *Moran*, is a place outside civilization and feminine moral rules, but Norris has progressed from that novel—he will make his man suffer for mastering the woman now, rather than rewarding him. The Ferriss's-door scene is a less bestial, more sophisticated version of the scene titled "A Battle" in *Moran*—but when that physical fight ends, Moran says, "you've conquered me, and ... I love you for it" (221). When this physical and moral fight ends, with Bennett forcing Lloyd to stop nursing his dying friend, she says, "You are not only killing him, you are killing my love for you" (*A Man's Woman* 131).

It is not quite as simple as this, for even here the woman enjoys being beaten down by a man's powerful love, as in *McTeague*; being bested by Bennett's strength, when he finally takes her in his arms, is a "glory," and she is "carried away in the rush of this harsh, impetuous, masculine power" (127). Then she says, "You must be brave for me now, and you must be strong for me and help me to do my duty" (129)—though the truth, as she'd said earlier, is that all she needs him to do is get out of her way! But after this brief celebration of feminine helplessness, Norris describes Bennett's beating her as a humiliation that wrecks her pride in herself.

And when Ferriss dies because he has forced her to leave him, Bennett feels humbled, too. He kneels at his friend's bed as if praying to him, and thinks: "Might it not have been avoided if he had been merely reasonable, as, in like case, an ordinary man would have been?" (168). Lynn is probably right that Norris saw his father as an exalted figure rather than an "ordinary man," so that man's own failure to be reasonable about his son's limitations is being fully confronted here for the first time. Fittingly, Bennett then gets typhoid himself, and Lloyd returns as his nurse, now stronger than he is. "This time you cannot make me leave," she says. "You shall do as I say! I have always carried my point, and I shall not fail now," he cries, but she lays him down like a child (190). It is an interesting rerun of the earlier scene, and Bennett's submission to love at its end, begging Lloyd not to leave him, is far better dramatized than Moran's. And it has an additional aspect, more relevant to the next chapter than this—for now, far from portraying Bennett as a father figure, Norris shows his relationship to Lloyd in a mother/son light.

So the middle novels end, having progressed, in Love's words, from "Ross Wilbur's moronic escapades" to "Bennett's carefully-planned polar exploring." But if Norris seemed to have to go "to the literal end of the earth" to find heroism in *A Man's Woman* (Love 14-5), he set his biggest image of Romance in his own state of California in his next novel. The men of *The Octopus* transcend Ward Bennett as well as Norris's earlier heroes, just as this book, his most ambitious effort, transcends all the others. It also has more examples of fathers and sons, both symbolic and actual, than any other. Though it is dominated by Annixter and Presley, who fit into neither category, Norris's original intention must have been to center the story on the family relationship, as shown by Magnus Derrick and his sons' places atop his list of characters. And there are also the previously-explored businessman-heroes, Cedarquist and Shelgrim, as well as the failed fathers, Dyke and Hooven.

Why does Norris put Magnus first, when Annixter's full awakening through Hilma's love is both a stronger plot and better related to the themes developed in the middle novels? He may have wanted simply to cast the dragon down once again. Magnus's name obviously suggests a large, heroic character, but perhaps one "magnified" rather than truly great. He, too, is a "Governor," but it is a title he never actually achieved. Lutwack, in his exploration of hero-types in *The Octopus*, sees him as a tragic king brought down by ambition (30). Norris probably did intend such a high Shakespearian plot, as his typically inflated early (a "commanding figure" compared to an officer of cavalry, plus Wellington) (*The Octopus* 626), and late (fat, sloppy and humiliated at length) descriptions show. But the story of the Derricks somehow never achieves this status.

One reason is that Magnus, even more than Jadwin, is planned as an illustration of the theme that gambling destroys men; thus he seems deflated to the "son" level of Norris-based gambling characters like Vandover and Condy. Another is that his wife, Annie, is not a "man's woman" at all, and can't protect him from failure. Richard Chase writes that Magnus symbolizes "the failure and decline of an older America" (193), and his frequent besting by people unhampered by morality—the blackmailing Genslinger, his own son Lyman—underlines this. Norris uses a familiar phrase, the "old school," to describe Magnus's origins, and the word "old" tells us that his is a generation that will not last. His moment of defeat, when he admits to his allies that the charges of bribery against him are true, occurs in an actress's feminized dressing room smelling of makeup, as if this man's aura of power had been only painted on. A few pages later, with the "stage" cleared of this lesser figure, the novel's true big patriarch, Shelgrim, makes his appearance.

The question of whether Shelgrim's voice in his "force" speech is Norris's has been discussed often. In fact, the scene seems less about force and more about Presley's need for a father, for someone who can answer his questions and soothe the uncertainty he feels about his impotence. He enters "the keep of the castle" in San Francisco to find the big man still at work after six, though 70 years old, and hearing the story of a drunken bookkeeper (*The Octopus* 1032). Instead of firing him, Shelgrim doubles his salary. This single example of how the commander deals with his underlings impresses Presley greatly; the wisdom of the action is debatable, but its image of boundless forgiveness reminds us again of a God. The famous speech ("The Wheat grows itself ... Can anyone stop the Wheat? Well, then no more can I stop the Road") (1036-7)—another example of Geary-like sheltering in naturalism—is actually nonsense. But the "stupefied" Presley, who is yet another parentless Norris character, is desperate for a patriarch and ready to believe anything Shelgrim says.

Although Ernest Marchand writes, "In other circumstances, Magnus might have been Shelgrim" (147), the big man—never seen to be a father himself, like his fellow "supermen" Bennett and Jadwin—has a much closer relationship to the novel's other childless warrior-hero, Cedarquist, than to the "old school" father who loses both of his sons. Like Norris, Lyman, corrupted by politics and the city, disappoints his father and is disowned; but then as a punishment, the man who thinks "he had but one son" after Lyman's betrayal (*The Octopus* 933) soon has none. Harran is killed in the ambush and the Derrick family disintegrates in failure. By contrast, Norris's largest patriarchs (except Vandover's father) never shrink from myth-father to actual-father status, just as his Great Mother characters never do.

Cedarquist's relationship to Shelgrim is actually a family one; his wife is related to the railroad magnate, who in turn donates money to her sham Renaissance—to keep the people entertained and docile, Cedarquist feels (828). Cedarquist's status as a Norris hero has already been described, but there is one more point worth noting: though he is present at the famous luxury-meal given while Mrs. Hooven starves in her "via dolorosa" scene, he's never mentioned in its descriptions. Norris, unable to accept this idealized "father" as sharing in the guilt, focuses instead on women (the "harpies" he condemns in his very effective cannibalism paragraph) and a feminized man, Julian Lambert.

The Hoovens are another example of a disintegrating family in *The Octopus* whose father cannot help. One may say that Hooven isn't to blame for their fate, since he is killed at the ditch as well; but Norris, in an even grosser portrayal of Germanic stereotypes than in *McTeague*, actually makes him responsible for the useless slaughter by having him cry out, "Hoch, der Kaiser! Hoch, der Vaterland!" and fire first (993). Left alone, the Hoovens go to the city—always a big mistake for Norris characters—where the mother dies and one daughter becomes a prostitute and the other presumably a ward of the State. Similarly, Norris creates a standard sentimental picture of the railroad engineer Dyke as a family head, doting on his daughter Sidney and supporting his aged mother. But Dyke's decision to rob a train and become a fugitive could hardly be made with his family's welfare logically in mind; and in the end he seems useless as both father and fighter, cut off by haste from seeing them or even delivering a final message, failing when he tries to shoot S. Behrman, and behaving like a trapped animal in his final struggle against capture.

Norris was sadly adept at creating characters who fail in their parental roles; even a minor character like Ida Wade's father in *Vandover*, who sells his "daughter's honor" in an out-of-court settlement with Vandover for $8,000 because it would "be enough to buy out his partner's interest, and even then he would have a little left over with which to improve a certain steaming apparatus" (190), shows this. *The Octopus* shows it even better. It has its archetype-sized male figures—Shelgrim, the "Durham bull," even the mythical Mexican leader Presley hears about in the first chapter ("He had the power of life and death over his people, and there was no law but his word") (593)—but none of them are visible fathers. The book's final parental image is of Magnus, now a dotard, and Annie, "listless, apathetic, calm," preparing to live in "Marysville" (1073), ironically choosing a town whose name is that of the greatest mother in Western tradition, even as their own lives as mother and father have effectively ended.

This leads us to *The Pit*, where Norris's own parents are fictionalized as people who never have a child. There is not much that is new in Curtis Jadwin—much of his author's career had already been devoted to rewriting the character of his own father. The main differences between Jadwin and someone like Cedarquist are the points, like his Sunday-school teaching and the details of his household, that are so clearly based on Frank Norris, Sr., and the ambivalence that clouds Norris's final attempt to create a myth-sized hero.

The Pit was seen as a "muck-raking" novel because it exposed those who profited at the expense of farmers and the hungry people who needed their produce; but Norris's efforts here were really bent toward showing how a great man could be belittled by a fatal flaw. As always, he chose gambling as the flaw. The "Napoleon of La Salle St.," who fights Chicago's "Battle of the Streets" in persistent war metaphors, is nonetheless imperfect—and Norris knows it, as when he has Jadwin desperately shout "It's a lie!" upon hearing of people starving in Italy because of the rise in the wheat price he's engineered (*The Pit* 320). The drive to gamble, to seek a Chance (the same capitalized idea Magnus follows) that will bring fortune, de-"magnifies" him as well. "It isn't so much the money as the fun of playing the game," says Jadwin (80); but the "fun" becomes an obsession that keeps him hooked even after his overwork makes him suffer strange Vandover-like nervous problems and headaches.

This comment by Alfred Kazin in *On Native Grounds* was named by Warren French as the inspiration for his Norris-as-moralist thesis: "the hold of the pit over Curtis Jadwin was exactly like the hold of drink over the good but erring father in a temperance novel" (101). A romantic and ultimately moral figure in Norris's eyes, but harmed by his addiction to gambling disguised as business, Jadwin is described very well by this phrase, "good but erring father." The first physical description of him in the novel, a Norman Rockwell image of the kindly American father, supports this view: "A heavy moustache touched with grey covered his lips. The eyes were twinkling and good-tempered" (*The Pit* 7).

Still, some critics seem themselves addicted to finding the Chicago Napoleon's flaws. Don Graham finds him "cliche-ridden and conventional," without the "sensuous romance" Laura wants to see in him (146)—perhaps this could also describe the elder Norris. Ziff thinks Jadwin's sexual energy, his "vital seed," is given to the Pit rather than to Laura (272); and French and Ernest Marchand see him as unable to grasp his success and his speculating intellectually. The latter view, though less racy, seems more penetrating. Curtis Jadwin may be large and commanding like Norris's other father-figures, but compared to men such as Bennett and Shelgrim, he is simply not very intelligent. His comment on the opera seen in Chapter One does much to reveal the cobwebs of sentimentality and middle-class "culture" filling his mind: "I would rather hear my old governor take his guitar and sing 'Father, oh father, come home with me now,' than all the fiddle-faddle, tweedle-deedle opera business in the whole world" (*The Pit* 24). (Notable also here are the familiar word "governor" for a father, and the hint of a temperance-novel tone in the song Norris chooses to mention.)

A rival "father" appears in this same chapter in the person of Cressler, who is "almost a second father to the parentless Dearborn girls" (13)—yes, Laura and her sister too are in the ranks of Norris orphans—and looks like that national father-figure, Lincoln. His is the anti-Pit voice in the novel, as when he says here, "the world's food should not be at the mercy of the Chicago wheat pit" (14). For all his Sunday-school teaching, Jadwin never shows such basic morality. Yet Norris destroys Cressler in the novel (he commits suicide after being ruined financially by Jadwin's speculating games) and makes Jadwin its hero.

Perhaps Cressler must fail because he's unable to grapple with the "force" which men like Shelgrim and Jadwin seek to master. But can they master it? Warren French's verdict on Shelgrim is that Norris was wrong in "the assumption that those who have the force and energy to put together an empire necessarily have the intelligence and patience to administer it adequately" (100). On the contrary, Norris probably did not hold this assumption; Presley, not the author, was fooled by Shelgrim, and Jadwin's lack of sufficient intelligence and patience is, as we've seen, clearly indicated by *The Pit*'s plot. Norris illuminates his "Force" better in this novel than anywhere else, with his symbol of the hellish, sucking Pit, and his description of the powerful male empire of Chicago, of which Laura thinks, "She was a little frightened—frightened of the vast, cruel machinery of the city's life, and of the men who could dare it, who conquered it ... must they not be themselves more terrible, more pitiless, more brutal?" (58). Perhaps Jadwin is simply not, in the end, pitiless and brutal enough.

Laura herself is a more complex character than Norris's other women, as shown in scenes such as her, "Ah, I was happy in those days—just a freckled, black-haired slip of a little girl," speech to Corthell, in which she's acting sadness and yet really sad. ("She was sincere and she was not sincere.") (281) The scene in which she gets bizarrely into costume for her husband and acts and dances for him as sole audience is also memorable, and instantly reminds us of Gertrude Norris, the frustrated actress. The extra shades of meaning in Laura as compared to Jadwin, whose similar sentimental memories—"I believe in making people happy ... But it's too late to do it now for my [dead] little sister" (190)—are presented without irony, probably appear because Frank Norris knew his mother better than he knew his father. Laura is a real person; her husband is an uncertain mix of realistic and romantic elements.

The man who truly fits with Laura is, as explained before, Sheldon Corthell. Laura describes Jadwin at first in the same words used about Bennett: "He didn't impress me as being a *woman's* man" (67). Mrs. Cressler answers deprecatingly that Corthell is just that; but to Norris, who so admired a "man's woman," this would make him superior, better able to transcend the dialectic than his rival. Laura later decides she loves Jadwin, but only after they have married and he's showered her with material rewards. As Graham (the critic who called Jadwin "cliche-ridden") writes, Corthell has more insight than Jadwin, and is not just the insulated dilettante that others see (150-1). In Laura, the artist stirs "unknown deeps ... for so long as he held her within his influence, she could not forget her sex a single instant" (*The Pit* 128). Later she thinks of Corthell, "He made her talk; he made her think" (340). Jadwin, a non-consummating "father" like Bennett and Shelgrim, stirs neither her mind nor her body; but for the reasons described already, he wins her anyway.

Ambivalent to the end of the novel, Norris notes in his conclusion that Jadwin's wheat-corner failure has made a great many people suffer, but Laura will see no blame in him. (And he is "like a father" to his protege Landry, who marries Laura's sister.) (399) Granville Hicks wrote that in *The Pit*

Norris "was unable to decide whether to regard Jadwin as hero, automaton, or villain" (174). This is true, but what this early critic failed to see is that the author had exactly the same uncertainty about his father. *The Pit* makes an appropriate last novel for Frank Norris. If he had lived to write *The Wolf* or the new trilogy he was planning, those books would certainly have included fathers, but no characters who summed up his torturous tangle of feelings toward his own father as well as Curtis Jadwin.

Of course there had to be more than one side to Frank Norris's double-bind. This issue of internal battle always raised its head in his writing, as in the "second self" motif and in this line describing Lloyd's feelings after being broken (temporarily) by Bennett: "Was not the struggle with one's self the greatest fight of all, greater, far greater, than had been the conflict between Bennett's will and her own?" (*A Man's Woman* 182). Norris faced his own "struggle with one's self" by writing again and again of the two sides of his upbringing represented by Lloyd and Bennett; but the mother-figure in his novels rose as far above congenital motherhood as the father-figure rose above physical fatherhood. And so, again, we begin the exploration of a gender with its archetype.

4

The Female Element:
Mothers and Great Mothers

FRANK Norris wrote about "supermen," but he also wrote about "superwomen." Unlike some other writers who worked to define masculinity and virility, such as London and Hemingway, he created women who were more than cardboard cutouts of trembling femininity to be protected, or worse, tempting Jezebels to be slapped aside. The previous sentence may describe the women of his short stories and early novels; but after his parents' divorce, Norris began creating characters like Lloyd and Hilma, who were fully capable of equaling, even mastering and molding their men. From the middle novels onward, he was less concerned with life-sized females (potential mothers, and thus potentially as troubling and bewildering as Gertrude had been to him), and more interested in what Jung called the "Great Mother."

As seen already, when we probe Jung's idea of the anima for its full meaning, we find no discrete meaning at all—just another definition of the mother. Man finds his "soul archetype," his anima, in his relationships with women, and the first and most powerful relationship is that of the infant to the life-giver. This is a physical reality. But Jung takes it farther than this, to the "ancestral experiences of the female" engraved in the unconscious, where "man carries within him the eternal image of the woman, not the image of this or that woman, but a definite feminine image" (17:198). It is the Eternal Feminine of Goethe's *Faust*—and, if we may compare the two works, of Norris's *The Octopus*.

The Great Mother, commonly known in one form as Mother Nature, is the unconscious, and to deny it carries both a practical (environmental damage) and spiritual price. Pizer sees this, rather than economic clashes, as the main theme of *The Octopus*. The book's male heroes gain new "values and belief following a perception of the meaning of the process of growth." Annixter and Vanamee—who are son-characters, incidentally, not father-characters like Magnus—learn transcendent truths from the wheat; the greedy ranchers and railroad don't (*The Novels of Frank Norris* 127, 144). In *The Pit* as well, Jadwin—another father-figure—tries to interfere with the wheat's laws, but is defeated. "As in *The Octopus*, the wheat fulfills its role as a benevolent world force in spite of those who try to impede its progress" (167).

Cargill and Marchand make the obvious point that without humanity, wheat could not be cultivated. But Norris probably agrees with Shelgrim on that one point: that the wheat is a libido-force and "grows itself." In *The Pit* it is described as "a primeval energy" raging against the "pinch of human spawn" (74); and Jadwin sees it just as his fellow father-hero does, as a force unto itself, advancing in yield by its own will to defeat him. Of course it's because he has raised the price that the farmers choose to grow more, but Norris likes this imagery too much to be logical.

In the previous chapter, the wheat's role as a male God was stressed, as when Presley thinks of its indifferent immensity compared to men, "Lilliputians, gnats in the sunshine" (*The Octopus* 934). But it is also a female God. It helps both Annixter and Vanamee to find love—"The earth, the loyal mother, who never failed, who never disappointed, was keeping her faith again" (870)—and it is described as being placed as a sexual "seed" in Mother Earth by the harvester. This latter idea probably came to Norris from Zola, but it is much older than any 19th-century author. The level earth is Yin (and the upthrusting mountain Yang) in China, and three Yin symbols in the I Ching mean earth (Clayre 202, 236). Jung also names a huge number of mother-symbols from human history, including ones like crosses and trees that are not relevant to Norris. But the "great womb of nature" idea certainly is.

Jung connects the womb, as noted before, to immortality, the healing of the original split from the mother. The "blending of the sensitive civilized man with nature is ... a reblending with the mother with whom we were truly and wholly one" (5:324). Paradoxically, this is also a death-wish. It is fitting that Bennett, in the Arctic, calls Adler's wish to stop marching and die "women's drivel" (*A Man's Woman* 26), for what this fierce, deadly form of nature represents *is* a woman—the other side of the "great" mother, the Terrible Mother. We return to her to be born again, but also to be re-absorbed, erased as individuals. The other novel of Norris's most relevant to this theme is *McTeague*.

One of the controversial aspects of this novel is what Norris called the "'death in the desert' business"—the increasingly romantic, even surreal events after Trina's murder, which Howells and others found jarring to the novel's pioneering realism. Pizer and Johnson found these scenes important to McTeague's role as an atavistic brute not at home in the city; as the latter critic wrote, "The strength and coarseness which are perverted in the city are quite adapted to the wilderness" ("The Frontier Behind Frank Norris's *McTeague*" 101). But McTeague *isn't* adapted any more, for we remember that he and Marcus foolishly kill themselves by fighting each other as their water drains away. Or is something other than the men themselves the agent of their deaths?

Dying of thirst is a totally appropriate end for McTeague; from the beginning of the novel the dentist (the symbolism of his profession is obvious) is an "oral personality." As Freedman's article describes, he feels great fondness for food and drink and is docile only when his hunger is satiated. He's even an oral sadist, biting Trina's fingers when angry (52, 55). Indeed, eating is a common event in the story; McTeague eats with Marcus often, his first social outing with Trina is a picnic, and the narrator dwells greatly on the orgy of eating at their wedding. When he's furious with Trina after leaving her, McTeague lies awake biting his mattress exactly as in Captain Jack's *Blix* description of hatred (*McTeague* 519).

It is when he is without a woman that the massive dentist, probably compensating for the loss of the nourishing mother, feeds and satiates his "brute" (as does Vandover) the most. Again, the excellent description of his life at the novel's beginning provides the details. "These were his only pleasures— to eat, to smoke, to sleep, and to play upon his concertina" (263). The predictable life of Polk Street—"a kind of run-down Eden," French calls it (64)—and the orally-centered routine of McTeague's Sundays both fulfill his needs and mark him as, like Vandover in his own laziness, a victim of the regression that Jung predicts for womanless men.

Unless man's libido "calls him forth to new dangers he sinks into slothful inactivity" (Jung 5:349)—in other words, lack of sexual progression (perhaps of child-bearing) leads to the opposite impulse: regression, return to the enveloping womb. Whenever man cannot adapt, or meet the demands of life, Jung writes, he is driven to regress to the prenatal. "The road of regression leads back to childhood and finally, in a manner of speaking, into the mother's body" (5:329). It is also a response to hunger and thirst, i.e. the desire for the lost breast (5:335). This perfectly fits both McTeague, at whose wedding feast "everything within reach of his hands found its way into his enormous mouth" (*McTeague* 382), and Vandover, who says of his substitute womb, the Imperial, "It's always pleasant and warm and quiet ... and you get such good things to eat" (*Vandover and the Brute* 35). Even the womanless expedition team of Bennett's is prone to this temptation: "To eat, to sleep, to be warm—they asked nothing better" (*A Man's Woman* 18).

All these details illustrate Jung's remark, "Were it not for the leaping and twinkling of the soul [the etymological root of "anima" is "soul"], man would rot away in his greatest passion, idleness" (9.1:27). But the inability to adapt to life, to emerge from childhood, is the problem which Vandover and McTeague especially have; and it is not surprising that they, like so many of Norris's characters, never have children. McTeague is essentially a child at the novel's beginning, and he tries at its end—after killing the failed mother-substitute, Trina—to go back even further, to the comforting Mother Nature in California's mountains and deserts.

Even before Trina's murder the novel's ending is telegraphed, when like Condy and Blix, McTeague takes long walks on San Francisco's sea-coast, "watching the roll and plunge of the breakers with the silent, unreasoned enjoyment of a child." Then he remembers the mines of his childhood: "In the stress of his misfortune McTeague was lapsing back to his early estate" (*McTeague* 495-6). So the final scenes are hardly as separate as some claim. After Trina's death McTeague does return to the mines, a setting completely different from the enclosing city, with immense mountains, growing trees, and as in *The Octopus*, "tremendous, immeasurable Life ... savage, sullen, and magnificently indifferent to man" (528). This is when McTeague's animal-life "sixth sense" of pursuit becomes a plot element.

But he can't escape. As Jung writes, the Terrible Mother usually ensures "that he who sought rebirth finds only death" (5:331). Marcus may be the father-punisher in part, but thirst, the denial of the female symbol of water, dooms him at the end as well. However, McTeague spares him this death by killing him; it is the enormous-mouthed protagonist himself who suffers that most orally-centered of fates at the hands of the true punisher, the Eternal Feminine.

The symbolism of Death Valley, "white, naked, inhospitable, palpitating and shimmering under the sun ... openly and unreservedly iniquitous and malignant" (*McTeague* 555, 560), is far from subtle. As George Spangler, in his article on the sexual themes in *McTeague*, puts it succinctly, it is a "symbolic expression of the destructive female principle" (56). Such exposures of the cruel side of Mother Nature appear elsewhere in Norris's novels, as in the tropical Pacific of *Moran*—"Everything was empty—vast unspeakably desolate—palpitating with heat" (122)—and the Arctic of *A Man's Woman*—"ice, ice, ice, fields and floes of ice, laying themselves out under that gloomy sky, league after league, endless, sombre, infinitely vast, infinitely formidable" (4-5). It is not surprising that a man who felt with such painful ambivalence the weight of his mother's hand on his life should have a strong mental image of what Jung calls the Terrible Mother.

People are born, according to Jung, with ancestral memories of which they are unconscious; and one form of this "curse" which parents may hand on is the Terrible Mother archetype (5:330). There are many forms of this archetype in myth—the bloody goddess Kali in India, the Mayan snake-headed goddess Ixchel, Oedipus's Sphinx, the Gorgon Medusa. She is the opposite of the nourishing mother of childhood; she devours the child to keep it from breaking away (Stevens 90-1). On a more individual level, this is a conflict which many suffer—among them Frank Norris. Jung writes: " ... whoever sunders himself from the mother longs to get back to the mother ... The mother then appears on the one hand as the supreme goal, and on the other as the most frightful danger—the 'Terrible Mother'" (5:236).

All of this makes the identity of Norris's familiar "Enemy" not as mysterious. We can see some manifestation of it in almost every novel: Vandover's horror when learning the details of childbirth; the Pacific's ill-treatment of Wilbur, drenching him with her waves and appalling him with her grey openness; the wheat punishing S. Behrman and Jadwin for challenging it. Only in *Blix* is nature kindly and womanhood pure without exception—this novel, of course, being about the relationship which helped Norris overcome the conflict described above.

Nowhere is this Enemy more dominant than in *A Man's Woman*.

McTeague is no match for "her"; he tries to deny feminine power by killing his wife, and is punished. (Even early in the novel he seems to foresee this doom, as he sings the one song he knows: "No one to love, none to caress,/Left all alone in this world's wilderness.") (*McTeague* 307) But Ward Bennett is another matter. The ice, not he, is the subject of *A Man's Woman*'s first sentence, as if to emphasize its power; it is "the Enemy ... the stupendous still force of a merciless nature, waiting calmly, waiting silently to close upon and crush him." But we still meet Bennett, as noted before, shaking his fist at it (as his jaw grows "salient") and vowing, "I'll break you" (5). Though Paul Bixler sees more Zola in *A Man's Woman* than in other Norris novels (114), the idea of man in an equal fight with nature, rather than being conquered by its indifferent strength, seems strongest here.

Furthermore, Bennett is not escaping into nature like McTeague, but confronting it from outside. Mother Nature may be "merciless" and playing the tricks described before to thwart him, but the explorer has come to the Arctic on his own initiative to "break" this adversary. No wonder Norris continues to use words like "cruel" and "merciless" to describe the wind and cold on the journey; Bennett is asking for punishment by committing the same crime the villains of the wheat novels do. He is trying to deny the power—ultimately, despite its sometimes brutal tactics, a unifying, benevolent power—of the Eternal Feminine.

Certainly Norris knows the terrible side of the Great Mother; his vivid descriptions of it help make the first two chapters of *A Man's Woman* the book's best. The wind outside the tent where Bennett's men are huddled, for instance, is "an enormous, mad monster gambolling there in some hideous dance of death"; and the landscape "gloomy, untamed, terrible, an empty region—the scarred battlefield of chaotic forces, the savage desolation of a prehistoric world" (32-3). This is not so much hostile nature as distorted nature; without warmth, there cannot be the bursting fertility that swells throughout *The Octopus*. Bennett's journey is one expression of his masculine- centered personality; he is deliberately cutting himself off from the life-giving mother, and in the love-story chapters with Lloyd, Norris as plot manipulator will show him how wrong he is. It is the same God (female, nourishing God in this case) v. science (cold masculine reason) form of Norris's dialectic mentioned earlier, as well as Jung's conscious-v.- unconscious form of it. Science is materialism, objectivity, denial of the unconscious—what Blake called "Newton's single vision." This is what Bennett represents, which is one reason he needs feminine tempering.

The unifying power of the Great Mother has already been described; as Jung, who saw the importance of "nirdvandva," pointed out, like the masculine "rta" or divine order, the elemental feminine transcends opposites. The first split is that from the mother—thus she symbolizes afterward the need for union (Jung 5:371). Such unity—reconciliation between good and evil, conscious and unconscious—is, to Jung and Norris as well, both possible and desirable. But Bennett, who sees the unconscious only as an "Enemy," cannot achieve it; as Norris describes him during his battle with Lloyd, "For him a thing was absolutely right or absolutely wrong, and between the two there was no gradation" (*A Man's Woman* 124). Lloyd, by contrast, sees "some strange affinity in all evil, as, perhaps, in all good" (163). An even greater affinity beyond good and evil is what Norris tries to achieve, successfully or not, at the end of his next novel, *The Octopus*.

Barbara Hochman calls *The Octopus* less "tidy" than the middle novels; death and birth are interrelated in it, as are good and evil (79-80). How is this possible? Nature is indifferent in this novel, but that word can be dissected to mean, not simply uncaring, but "not different"—free from opposites. As Jung put it: "In itself the world is indifferent. It is my Yes and No that create the differences" (6:191). This Yes and No, Yang and Yin—whatever we call duality in its many forms—are what Norris always worked to reconcile before, but especially in, the wheat novels. Now married to Jeannette and thus shielded from the impulse to regression which threatens his early male characters, Norris was able to attempt this reconciliation, even if many critics aren't convinced. Now he added to the tall, blonde women who had helped his earlier heroes (represented here by Hilma, who finally is even "unusually, almost unnaturally tall") (*The Octopus* 1079), an even larger female figure: the Great Mother.

In a cross-definition typical of Jung, he writes that nature *is* the mother; man is conscious and not part of nature (the unconscious, the anima), but we have a love for Mother Nature that represents our love for the ideal mother (5:323). Of course not all men, or all of Norris's characters, love nature, and this is the root of conflict in his later novels. The tension is seen when Hilma, that child of nature and Great Mother in her own right, is gathering watercress by a creek. The railroad line runs past it, so that the creek's sound is often "interrupted by the thunder of trains roaring out upon the trestle overhead ... leaving in the air a taint of hot oil, acrid smoke, and reek of escaping steam" (*The Octopus* 834). It is the same clash of symbols as in the well-known scene where an engine runs into a flock of sheep; the sheep represent not the human victims of the railroad, but the benevolent "natural dynamism" of the wheat, which men like Magnus, S. Behrman, and (until Hilma reforms him) Annixter deny.

The planting imagery in *The Octopus*—the earth delivering the "fruit of its loins" after being seeded with the "long stroking caress, vigorous, male, powerful" of the plow (586, 680)—is as sexual as Norris gets. Even his description of the rape of Angele Varian is worded vaguely, but this writer who could generally only hint at sex between actual men and women had no problem detailing the union of the "elemental Male and Female" in nature. Hilma, though described sensually, is more a Female with a capital F than an actual woman dwarfed by realism. The first rain of the season occurs on the day she's introduced in the novel, and just as the earth, drinking in the rain, is called "redolent with fertility," Hilma at work in the dairy is "redolent and fragrant with milk" (672, 709).

It is a different nature from that with which the violent early characters, McTeague and Moran, are identified. It seems that after separating from his own mother, Norris was better able to visualize the Great Mother—who, like "Tian" and the archetypal father, represents the comforting unity of divine law (or the libido). Even in his essay on "The Mother Archetype" Jung generalizes so much that it seems virtually anything can be a mother symbol, but most of his choices emit fertility or fruitfulness: a creative female deity. The belief in God as everywhere in nature was common in Norris's time, not only because of his precursor Emerson, but as Pizer points out, in Spencer and a popular book called *Through Nature to God* (*The Novels of Frank Norris* 7). This theme develops in Norris just as Pizer tells us: from men succumbing to bestiality to man allying himself with nature and God.

Nature is always a punishing God, as when she sinks Captain Kitchell to protect Moran or subjects Bennett's expedition to "infinite" hardship. But in *The Octopus* this role softens. Of course there is S. Behrman's death, which some critics think is contrived and could have happened to anyone; but in fact he has the ship's hold filled with the wheat in which he will drown because he doesn't want to pay 4 cents apiece for bags, and he steps into the hold's doorway to look at the wheat and enjoy his triumph (1088). (The inability of Dyke and Presley to kill the villain clearly happens so he can be saved for this deified death.) Outside of this vengeance, however, nature is kind in *The Octopus*, the wheat a feminine nourisher and symbol of love and immortality—as Father Sarria says, quoting a wheat-metaphor passage from St. Paul as evidence.

Nature has smaller but still significant roles in the other novels. In *Vandover*, as befits an early novel, it simply gives the hero a lesson in cold force via the shipwreck incident. In *Blix*, the San Francisco coast and the fishing-site countryside represent something greater and freer than the social world marked by, as Don Graham points out, bad-taste interiors (12). Finally, though *The Pit* is a wheat novel, nature's part in it is seen most in the Chicago weather, notably rain and snow. Rain often falls on grim events in the novel, such as the day Jadwin hatches his doomed plan to corner the wheat, and, significantly, the day of his and Laura's wedding. In all seven novels, whatever her different shades of countenance, we meet the Earth Mother, the goddess of fertility and dispenser of nourishment.

Motherhood is more than joyful green shoots of wheat, however; its negative side is part of life, and of Norris's works. This side occurs not only in the hugeness of the Terrible Mother archetype, but in the life-size psychology of the mother-complex. Jung's belief in a "secret conspiracy" in some mother-son relationships has already been mentioned, but the mother-complex is a broader idea than this. The longing for the mother is an infantile need; the mother-child relationship is obviously our most powerful, since for some time the child is a part of the mother's body. But beyond that, the longing may become an "aching inner emptiness" which cannot be forgotten (Jung 8:369). Primitives deal with this by creating spirits, he writes, but modern man by creating neuroses.

Did Frank Norris have such a neurosis, and can it be seen in his work? Jung felt that this complex could be exposed by early death, an over-attention to "bold and resolute manliness," the Don Juan syndrome of passing from woman to woman, or homosexuality (9.1:87). Some of these details point clearly to Norris or his characters, while others do not. Vandover is something of a "Don Juan," as well as having an over-attachment to the image of his dead mother; Norris probably behaved similarly, as Walker hints. The presence of homosexuality in Norris's novels is hard to detect. Feminine-named Dolly Haight, never seen to pursue women as his friends do, is a possible candidate; but a general interest in the female as substitute mother or genteel-tradition helpmate, rather than as sexual partner, is the basic attitude of a Norris man. Our chief hint about the mother-complex here is an elementary fact of psychology: that the more fiercely a person denies something, the less we can trust this denial.

A masculine, rational character like Bennett brushes the Great Mother furiously aside, naming her the "Enemy." But the regression wish isn't an external enemy—it's the inner longing for death which appears so often (in female form) in literature: the call of the Sirens, Longfellow's Hiawatha sailing off willingly to death, Poe's A. Gordon Pym courting death throughout his novel and finally meeting a huge, perhaps female figure where the oceans of the world rush together. And Moran's corpse floats out on her boat "to the great gray Pacific that knew her and loved her ... enfolded her, held her close, and drew her swiftly, swiftly out to the great heaving bosom" (*Moran of the Lady Letty* 291-2). These words show how well Norris knew the pull of this longing. But he denied it as angrily as most of his male characters do. The absence of successful motherhood is one of the most consistent motifs in the plots of his novels.

It is easy to draw the conclusion that Norris's invisible or absent mothers condemn his own mother. Jung wrote that a failure on the part of the individual mother led to a greater leaning on the larger mother image (8:372). This is what Norris seems to have done by turning more and more to the mother archetype, rather than to actual mothers, as he wrote his novels. But does he protest too much? In his earliest completed novel, *Vandover*, the hero has an exalted image of his lost parent: he imagines her in Heaven as quoted before, and sees her as "some kind of an angel ... so sweet, so good and so pure" (8)—an ideal which is shattered when he learns about sex and childbirth. Yet still he idealizes women as art objects in pictures like his "Flora." *Vandover*, we remember, was born in part from Norris's fear and guilt about disappointing his own parents; here as elsewhere—for example, in giving Condy a living mother but one we never see, or in his entire presentation of Laura Jadwin—what we find in Norris is not total rejection, but agonizing ambivalence.

Vandover's final, unrealized ambition as an artist is to paint "The Last Enemy." Though death is visualized in this painting as male (a lion), the use of the word "Enemy" throughout *A Man's Woman*, and a momentary reference in *Moran*—"this last enemy was the girl he loved" (218)—are clues that Norris really had the luring womb of the Terrible Mother in mind. This devouring symbol of the unconscious is fulfilling the secret desire of the son to be sucked back in—and Norris, like any man who senses this desire in himself, feared it. Yet to leave the mother is also to confront the fear of death, since nature has no more use for us after we procreate and fulfill our adult role. And ironically, Frank Norris actually did die soon after his marriage and fatherhood. Yet in the end he probably escaped the "retrospective longing," the unconscious wish to return to the womb, which Jung believed is the true danger in the Terrible Mother (5:390).

Norris put both the Great and Terrible maternal archetypes, though neither he nor anyone else had yet identified them, into his work. His final novels, through the wheat and other plot elements, show a larger appreciation at the end of his life for the Great archetype than fear of her devouring twin sister. When he writes lyrically about the pregnant Hilma as "the Mother" surrounded by love, or shows the growing wheat planting the "seed" of love in Annixter, it is Carl Jung's "lovingly tender ... joyous and untiring giver of life" that he invokes (9.1:92).

Gertrude Norris and Her Son

As the young lovers in *Blix* walk along the sea, Norris states the central point of his literary credo more directly than in any other novel. "Life was better than literature. To live was better than to read; one live human being was better than ten thousand Shakespeares; an act was better than a thought. Why, just to love Blix ... was better than the best story, the greatest novel he could ever hope to write. Life was better than literature, and love was the best thing in life" (228).

It seems that Norris is truly rejecting his mother's old artistic ambitions for him here. In fact, only in *Blix* does he reveal the dreariest, loneliest aspect of writing, the work itself. In the next chapter after this scene of freedom with his loved one, Condy is shown plodding away at his *Moran*-like adventure story, a prisoner of the solitary profession Norris's mother wished him to follow. He is compared to a galley-slave, and feels "all the pain, the labor, the downright mental travail and anguish that fall to the lot of the writer of novels" (239). Though this "anguish" is never described in the literary essays, it's not strange that this should be the attitude of a man who admired and attempted to pursue strenuous-life sporting activities, and who, Franklin

Walker tells us, "was never a writing man when he was away from his desk" (282). Maternal "literature" may have finally beaten male "life" in the story of Frank Norris, but he made his disdain for the victor clear.

There is hardly a more appropriate novel in which he could have done this. If the middle novels are a transition in his fiction, *Blix* is the fulcrum of the trio, with the backward-looking *Moran* and its sexless violence on one side, and the forward-looking *A Man's Woman* and its love-softened hero on the other. This is also appropriate. The events in this romantic-genre novel, usually tossed aside as slight and immature by critics, are a retelling of what was actually the most important and maturing experience of Frank Norris's life: finding a wife. In the passage quoted above, the "life" side of the dialectic is, for once, not equated with manly actions, but with love—specifically, love of Jeannette Black. No wonder Norris states such anti-writing feelings here; he *would* rather love the real-life "Blix" than please his mother with artistic achievements.

The tension between a man's wish to stay united with his mother, and his need to love a woman who will share his own children, is one of the central issues of male psychology. Jung wrote of mother-longing, but also of the importance of adult sexual love. For him, man "finds his mother in the woman he loves" (5:332)—or just as commonly, though the great psychologist may not see it, finds a needed *opposite* to his mother in her. It is not an easy battle to win. A mother almost always clings to her child, perhaps more so if her marriage is unsatisfactory, as was Gertrude Norris's. To break free from the tightest bond and give up his first love, the son needs "a faithless Eros," to prevent which the mother "has carefully inculcated into him the virtues of faithfulness, devotion, loyalty" (Jung 9.2:12)—or carefully read novels to him, encouraged his dabbles in painting, and fought against her husband's attempts to make him a second-generation jeweler.

Frank Norris did succeed in finding his own partner, but he had to acknowledge the sexuality he condemned in his earlier novels to do it. Probably his description of sexual attraction and marriage as something bestial and entrapping in *McTeague* was connected to the successful implantation of the "virtue of loyalty" to his mother. To marry, a man must conquer any fear of sex and turn from the mother to find a "receptive female" in the world beyond her (Stevens 130). After Norris did this, his themes naturally changed; sex was no longer McTeague's "sewer" but Hilma's curvy, milky body, and the most visible mother was the Great Mother. This latter point is also because mother-longing is never completely overcome. A wife fills the void in part, but the wish for the lost mother then becomes concentrated in the archetypal mother—as in Norris's great nourisher, the wheat.

Before Jeannette, Frank Norris was nearly as attached to his mother's image and appalled by sex (as an attachment to other women) as was Vandover. As the oldest of Gertrude's three sons, and probably the main repository of the wishes left empty after one of them died, Frank must have seemed to her a natural ally against her partner in an increasingly bad marriage. It is not surprising that Frank's brother Charles also became a novelist—their mother's appreciation for art was a strong force, so that neither surviving son became the businessman-heir Frank, Sr. hoped for.   No description of the young Norris supports Lynn's tag of "bookish and shy"; he admired soldiers and athletes and enjoyed fraternity life.   But the double-bind was already in place before his parents' divorce, and the brute-v.-refinement dialectic so prevalent in *Moran* and elsewhere was already pulling at him. He never forgot the upper-class handsomeness of his mother, as seen in Laura Jadwin or in the "ladies from the great avenue a block above Polk Street ... beautifully dressed ... gloved and veiled and daintily shod" (*McTeague* 267)— one of whom was Gertrude Norris—who shopped daily in McTeague's neighborhood.

This is the root of the artistic-taste theme that Don Graham spends an entire book detailing. However he tries to distance himself from Gertrude in his novels, even in *Blix*, Frank, Jr.'s appreciation of her fine New England sensibilities—as opposed to Frank, Sr.'s bourgeois commercialism—is evident.   Graham sees the growth of the novel's hero and heroine as "an education in aesthetic perception" (12), a perception whose lack, however much he posed at rough-edged manliness, Norris always condemned. Early in the novel he describes the Bessemers' standard middle-class family parlor: a piano nobody ever plays, pictures of John Alden and Priscilla, and even the "bisque fisher boy" that symbolizes dull realism in his literary essays (118). It is within this setting that Condy thinks grimly of his bloodless "Younger Set" life, in which he knows only the Travis Bessemer of dinner parties and afternoon functions. "Had they played out the play, had they come to the end of each other's resources?" (119). They haven't—but they must leave this room and what it represents to learn that. Later, they argue in the same setting about his clothes' bad taste and her house's bad taste; and immediately afterward is a description of San Francisco as seen from her window, ending in "a vast, illimitable plane of green—the open Pacific" (158), a great-maternal symbol that offers them a larger horizon.

Bad taste is everywhere in Norris's novels. Norris the painter satirized popular, Curtis Jadwin-level artistic awareness by including nearly identical scenes in *Vandover* and *McTeague* where the characters ignorantly visit an art fair. (Trina even speaks the classic cliche, "I'm no critic, I only know what I like.") (*McTeague* 402) There is also the theatre scene in *McTeague*, where the lowbrowed dentist and Mrs. Sieppe laugh uproariously at inane stage antics and McTeague thinks: "Art could go no further" (334).

But rooms, as in *Blix*, is what Norris dwells on most—Ida Wade's Bessemer-style bourgeois house in *Vandover*; McTeague's "Dental Parlors," and then his and Trina's apartment with its absurd pictures of children dressed as adults (a symbol of these characters as they try to embark on a mature life?); the residential room where Lloyd assists in a hip operation in *A Man's*

Woman, with its everyday details "trivial, impertinent" compared to this battle with death (56); the feminized, possession-cluttered home that Hilma makes of Annixter's ascetic rooms; the huge house where Laura roams alone in *The Pit*. The few tasteful exceptions are interesting. Corthell's apartment, artistically balanced and full of paintings, contrasts with Vandover's self-indulgently furnished studio to suggest that Norris approves of Corthell and considers him something of a successful Vandover. And three whole paragraphs in *The Octopus* describe a room of "faultless taste"—but it's the room in which the luxurious meal takes place while Mrs. Hooven starves (1049).

Norris, tutored by his mother, could tell good taste from bad and wished to show this off; but the last example points out his familiar ambivalence. Mrs. Cedarquist, in part one of Norris's satiric portraits of his mother, throws French—the language of culture and of the country where Gertrude Norris's son studied art—into her conversation as she hosts Presley and the effeminate Lambert at this meal. Graham believes that Mrs. Cedarquist's circus of artistic fakers included portraits of some of Norris's own acquaintances (68); if so, he must have felt uneasy at associating with people who represented his mother-dominated side.

Frank Norris was almost as frightened of femininity in himself as of the outsized femininity of the Terrible Mother. It is Mrs. Cedarquist's protege, Hartrath, who says, "Beauty unmans me" (*The Octopus* 827); and Ross Wilbur, emasculated by his debutante-ball world at the outset of *Moran*, jokes—maybe without joking—that he's "afraid of girls" and their company "unmans me" (5). No man is described as feminine more often than that symbol of Norris's sexual guilt and fear, Vandover. He is "almost feminine" in shame at his first one-night stand, is "as careful as a woman in the matter of dress," feels "feminine weakness" after his father dies, and keeps trying to paint out of "feminine caprice" (*Vandover and the Brute* 18, 19, 117, 169). Particularly of note is his "veritable feminine horror of figures" (218-9), since it was Norris's own weakness with figures (whether genuine or unconsciously magnified) that kept him from pleasing his father by graduating from Berkeley.

Yet Norris found much to admire in his mother, however uncertain about his own manliness her victory made him feel. The strength of the "superwomen" in his middle novels is partly inspired by her strength. Norris was certainly no feminist, but there is a "new woman" quality to Moran, Blix and Lloyd; Ernest Marchand, who also finds Moran "a memorable creation," uses the phrase about these heroines (116), just as Ahnebrink does about Norris's mother. Ahnebrink finds the frontier West's women as strong as its men, and Moran "emancipated ... completely free from convention" (225-6).

That large-fisted Viking is not, however, the best example of Norris's respect for emancipated women; in fact, she *is* trapped in convention—the conventions of the adventure novel that Norris felt he must follow to earn money for Jeannette. It is Blix and the heroines that follow her who illustrate this new-woman theme best. Blix wants to go to New York to study medicine, because "why shouldn't I have a profession just like a man—just like you, Condy? ... isn't studying medicine, Condy, better than piano-playing, or French courses, or literary classes and Browning circles? Oh, I've no patience with that kind of girl!" (*Blix* 207). When Condy makes the myopic remark that she might find someone to marry in New York, she protests, "No; I'm going there to study medicine" (208).

Critics love calling the characters in *Blix* immature—a typical comment is Oscar Cargill's, "If the book has any merit, it is its complete naivete, but surely it ought not to be praised for this" (93). It is part of Norris's plan to have Condy immature, and small details like Blix catching six fish and him catching none when they go fishing show how Norris makes fun of his autobiographical hero. Debra Munn has aided our understanding of *Blix* considerably by comparing the magazine text to the published book. The role of Blix as surrogate mother becomes even clearer as her personality changes from "a wonder of patience, consideration, and sensitivity" in the magazine to "a candidate for sainthood" in the novel; Condy, by contrast, becomes even more of a childish buffoon in Norris's revision, as in the revealing change of "Blix, I wish I was a better sort of chap" to "Blixy, wish I was a better sort of chap" (Munn 52, 53). Perhaps the line toward the end of the novel, "Oh, Blixy, little girl, do *you* love *me*?" (*Blix* 267) was similarly altered. But any assertions by critics, or by Blix herself (when she admits she loves Condy, she claims to have been "just a girl ... not very serious" before) (273), that the woman in the couple are naive are denied by her command of her motherless family and her medical-school plans.

Lloyd Searight is even stronger, an older Blix who has completed her schooling and become a nurse. Though she hides the fact and acts as an equal to her colleagues, she founded the nursing "agency" where she works; and this professional success, plus her firmly independent stand toward Bennett, mark her as the most liberated of Norris's women. Yet Norris, in the midst of painting this admirable portrait, is struck by his old fear of domination by the feminine and must include frequent, inconsistent lines in *A Man's Woman* about female weakness. "Was it a mistake, then? Could a woman be strong?" thinks Lloyd as the explorer confronts her at Ferriss's door; and when she admits to the head nurse that she was forced by male power to leave her patient, she responds that "men are stronger than women, Lloyd" (120, 161).

Norris's ambivalence about gender finally mars both *Blix* and *A Man's Woman*. Even in the midst of her career plans, Blix says that her aunt thinks of medicine as a "woman's profession," and that she'll go to a college for women to pursue it. "I hate a masculine, unfeminine girl as much as you do," she tells Condy (207). And Norris has Lloyd quit her profession when she marries Bennett, becoming little more than a Penelope waiting at home for the manly conquerer. Her "man's woman" career is "to be his inspiration, his incentive, to urge him to the accomplishment of a great work ... renunciation, patience ... to wait in calmness for its issue—that was her duty; that the woman's part in the world's great work" (*A Man's Woman* 207, 209). Thus the author denies all the apparent feminism he's presented before!

As the picture of Norris as a self-conscious "master in his own house" reminds us, he was uncertain even when gratefully accepting Jeannette's love about whether men and woman should be equal. To admit this equality might have seemed to be admitting his own weakness in living the life his mother, not his father, chose. Debra Munn calls *Blix* "Norris's fictionalized version of how he finally grew out of a protracted adolescence with the help of a real-life 'man's woman'" (47). This is an accurate description, and yet Norris still could not totally avoid stumbling through treacherous fields of opposites. His union with Jeannette was truly an escape from the sort of too-close relationship which Jung felt blocked the individual's development. But Jung also wrote that "the conscious mind of the son demands separation from the mother, but his childish longing for her prevents this by setting up a psychic resistance" (5:297). Norris showed his fragments of resistance by denying, to the end, the possibility of a partnership in which both genders are strong and support one another.

In the last two years of Norris's life, he had almost solved the paternal side of his old dilemmas; he was past the financial (if not emotional) consequences of his disinheritance, and had found the woman who would help him become a father rather than a dependent son. This marriage, at a time when his mother was still trying to exert a hold on him, offered a solution to the maternal pull as well—but not a complete solution. Jung states a theme familiar outside his writings as well, that the marriage choice is influenced, either positively or negatively, by the parents. Children are driven unconsciously in a direction to compensate for what their parents didn't have (17:191). He also believed that a son overly bound to his mother will marry an inferior or tyrannical woman—but there is certainly no evidence that Jeannette Black was either. We are reminded here of Dolly Haight's marriage proposal likening a wife to a sister or, naturally, a mother; but Jung and Norris, if not Dolly, knew that heterosexual love was the chief aspect of marriage. The psychologist's description of sex sounds like another solution to Norris's many dualities: "Normal sex life as a shared experience with apparently similar aims further strengthens the feeling of unity and identity. This state is described as one of complete harmony, and is extolled as a great happiness (one heart and one soul) since the return to that original condition of unconscious oneness is like a return to childhood" (17:192).

Perhaps, then, his marriage finally satisfied the guilty struggles within Frank Norris about sex. What Dillingham called his "Destructive Women" appear mostly in the early novels; the punishments in *Vandover* and *McTeague*, from V.D. to "death in the desert," disappear during the middle novels. The later Norris did nothing so blatant as, for example, presenting the fleshless geriatric union of *McTeague*'s Old Grannis and Miss Baker as the only successful coupling in that novel, their meeting "[l]ike two little children ... awkward, constrained, tongue-tied with embarrassment" (345) keeping them free of that "sewer" of sexual desire. Yet the uncertainty always remained. Moving on past the completely implausible love-story in *Moran* through the adolescent "chum" relationship in *Blix*, Norris finally reached the wheat novels—but even here, he could not detail sex except in agricultural terms. The author's often-noted prudishness remained in such details as Hilma finding the bed she buys with Annixter a luxury and a "wonder," but never thinking of making love in it (*The Octopus* 899); Laura's discomfort with Corthell's appealing to her sexually and her choice, instead, of a man who apparently does not; and the vague hints that leave it unclear whether these two have committed adultery or not.

Frederic Cooper stated that Norris was too young to write the wheat books (323), and although he didn't mean it in this sense, the author really was not ready, as a very new husband, to tell the full story of male-female union that many European writers have told so well. Norris inherited some of this outlook from the century of his birth, the genteel-tradition belief in woman as Christ (Pizer, "The Masculine-Feminine Ethic in Frank Norris's Popular Novels" 89); in fact Jadwin says in *The Pit*, "I believe in women as I believe in Christ," as part of his marriage proposal to Laura (118). Jadwin, like other Norris men, can see a woman only as a moral guide, not a partner in bed (of course, Norris may have also found it hard to imagine his parents in this role, even in fiction). But beyond that genteel influence, even a married Norris found the idea of adult physical love, a powerful declaration of the son's independence, difficult to set down positively on paper.

Blix is not completely de-sexualized, as shown by its references to "feminine perfume," and to the heroine's "little triangle of white skin, that was partly her neck and partly her cheek, and that Condy knew should be softer than down, smoother than satin, warm and sweet and redolent as new apples" (205); but Blix's dressing with her neck "swathed high and tight in white" on the fishing trip (178) sends a different message, and the narrator himself notes near the novel's end that the young "chums" don't think of sex. Then there is finally a small consummation, as they kiss each other—Norris uses the three simple words, "on the mouth," here, as compared to "grossly, full on the mouth," the phrase used twice in *McTeague*. However, we cannot tell whether the author has really changed his ideas, or is surrendering to the necessity of fulfilling popular romantic-novel expectations.

But this novel retains its significance as Norris's public retelling of his transition from the "secret conspiracy" to an apparently normal marriage. This is seen in its satirical pokes at his mother in the "Browning circles" reference, which editor James Hart's note tells us was one of Gertrude Norris's activities, and in the character of K.D.B., whose "respectability encased her like armor plate, and ... never laughed without putting three fingers to her lips" (254-5), and who acts educated but is actually reading the Encyclopedia volume by volume. It's seen in Blix's freeing Condy from that all-purpose vice, gambling, while his mother does nothing (he goes out to gamble once because his mother is "not to be home that evening") (210); in her role as general parent to the Bessemer family, with its dead mother and distracted father; in her prodding Condy's dormant ambition with lines like "you must make up your mind that you will go East, and then set your teeth together and do it" (209), making him quite different from McTeague, who was raised to his profession by his mother's will; and especially in the ironic, guilty dedication of the novel: "To My Mother."

Blix, like Lloyd (*A Man's Woman* was also written after Norris and Jeannette's courtship), is the ideal picture of a "man's woman"—as in the preceding novel, the actual phrase is used, when Condy exclaims, "You're a *man's* woman, that's what you are" (248). Earlier, he says, "You could put life into a dead man. You're the kind of girl that are the making of men" (210), and perhaps Jeannette *did* "make" the adult Frank Norris—a nearly mature writer, freed from the conventional social set and rules which his mother tried to lock him into (and which all the middle-novel heroines despise). But he exaggerated his gratitude by drowning the character of Blix in adjectives of praise—"She was just a good, sweet, natural, healthy-minded, healthy-bodied girl, honest, strong, self-reliant, and good-tempered" (108)— and making Condy an absurd child.

Walker notes that Condy, in a less desperate way than Vandover, is a dramatization of Norris's weaknesses at the time; his "lack of determination and set purpose" is a trait the writer recognized in himself (147). The problem is that Norris makes him so foolish that even the best "man's woman" might not have improved him: a hack writer with a "smooth-shaven and pink face" and tasteless clothes (*Blix* 115), always awkward and blundering, reciting an idiotic limerick and saying, "Suppose we break something—just for fun," when he and Blix visit a Chinese restaurant (145). He is so childish that, as Debra Munn points out, he "seems to need a mother more than a fiancee" (52). This not only creates unbalanced character development, where Condy changes but Blix does not, but it distorts the real story of a man moving onward *from* his mother. A few more simple symbols such as the couple's fishing preparations, in which Condy tangles everything together and Blix untangles it, would have made the novel better than this heavy-handed picture of a stumbling post-adolescent and the much younger "candidate for sainthood" who reforms him.

But Norris could not have written such a novel, because his love for its model, and his appreciation for her widening his horizons and partly freeing him from the clashing of his dialectic, was so strong. Jung saw sex as "a genuine and incontestible experience of the Divine" (17:192). The Frank Norris who was bound to his mother described such desire as "the smudge of a foul ordure, the footprint of the monster" (*McTeague* 284); but a reading of *Blix* and the novels that follow it shows that after discovering the partner of his life's few remaining years, he found it divine as well.

The Women of the Novels

Norris's feminine figures show even more ambivalence, and are of even more different types, than his masculine figures. Instead of the son and the father, we see when examining his women an array of potential and actual mothers ranging from completely weak, failed ones to full embodiments of the anima. Jung saw the actual mother as important only in terms of the maternal archetype; this belief in a "dual mother," both real and symbolic, an individual woman blended with an unconscious image of eternal motherhood, was central to his theories. Norris, however, was not able to blend these images. His mother-figures, when not Great or Terrible, are hardly mothers at all, either because their children die or because they are of no use to their living children. The final category, absent mothers, is the ultimate negation, the product of the author's tendency to sink from ambivalence into simple despair.

Like all aspects of Norris's novels, his female characters reveal the wish to unite his "Yes and No that create the differences." The old life-v.-literature struggle is always there, so that a character like Moran represents the temptation toward primitive manliness, an escape from the over-refinement that Gertrude's son saw in her world, just as much as a character like McTeague does. And here, as when examining his male figures, we see the transition from the years of divorce and disinheritance, when his hope of pleasing both parents seemed to have failed, through the restless searching of the middle novels, to the final (if not unobscured) glimpses of "nirdvandva" found in his marriage. But the categories of women cut along different lines than mere chronology. Frank Norris wrote not so much about dual motherhood as multiple motherhood.

The man Lynn thought of as a "mama's boy" wrote his first novel about a true mama's boy, Vandover. This long cry of apology to Norris's parents starts with an image which is both a punishment for Van and a hanging-in-effigy of Gertrude Norris: the ignominious death of his mother. A train journey has further lowered the condition of this presumably sickly woman, and now, weak, pale, and perspiring, "she drew a long sigh, her face became the face of an imbecile, stupid, without expression, her eyes half-closed, her mouth half-open. Her head rolled forward as though she were nodding in her sleep, while a long drip of saliva trailed from her lower lip" (*Vandover and the Brute* 4). This revolting picture is said to be Vandover's only memory of her—yet the first chapter also tells of the saintly maternal image he cherishes. Thus the very first mother in Norris's novels shows his mingled love and fury.

As in *McTeague*, with Norris's feelings of guilt and anger at his parents' divorce probably then at their height, sex and physical motherhood are looked upon here with disgust. Vandover first hears the word "childbirth," ironically, in a church sermon, and wonders at it until "one day he heard the terse and brutal truth. In an instant he believed it, some lower, animal intuition in him reiterating and confirming the fact ... The whole of his rude little standard of morality was lowered immediately. Even his mother, whom he had always believed to be some kind of an angel, fell at once in his estimation" (8). The intrusive narrator tells us that this "brutal truth" is the reason Van is able afterward to pursue cheap one-night stands with women. Though Stanley Cooperman points out correctly that such passages fit the American tradition of "Calvinist-Christian-guilt" in which nature is sin (253), we can see the personal wish to reject even the essence of motherhood in a man who, now studying writing at Harvard with his approving mother gazing on, felt that femininity had conquered him.

Yet at the same time he was terrified at losing his mother as he had lost his father, and Van, like McTeague, suffers this loss (or rather it's reported) on the first page of his story. In response Van mothers himself, as Barbara Hochman tells us (46), and as revealed in such details as his spending two to three hours in the bath every day, and showing his taste for luxury and warmth by building his room around the "famous tiled stove." The motherless McTeague does exactly the same thing with his Sunday steam beer and concertina. Vandover suffers losses throughout the novel, but the most interesting in this context is the loss of his ability to draw or paint. For here, the son becomes himself a failed mother. His fingers have suffered "impotency," so that he can finally draw only "changelings, grotesque abortions," the "hideous spawn" of the brute within him; this loss of ability feels to him "like the death of a child of his" (*Vandover and the Brute* 169, 172).

Norris was right not to kill off Vandover as he did McTeague; this allows the novel's appropriate last scene—in which his now totally alone, totally punished alter ego faces a complete family when he cleans their home—to close with the powerful image of the motherless neo-child facing the true child who has a mother (and is eating bread, a small example of his nourishment by the Great Mother). Vandover can never clean away, as his always finding more hideous muck under the family's sink symbolizes, the stain of sexual guilt that the 24-year-old Norris saw in himself. But Norris rejects procreation even more savagely in *McTeague*, a novel celebrated for its realism but in fact ultimately surreal, as George Spangler's article details, in its murderous greed and hatred that all proceeds from female sexuality.

Earlier critics might have believed, as Norris did, that he was following Zola's credo of heredity in this novel. But the evil of hundreds of generations that taints McTeague is an idea from the world of hellfire preachers, not of naturalism. More recent readers like Spangler and Walter Benn Michaels, plus our own understanding of Norris's inner conflicts, show that this novel was really a lower-class, more violent retelling of the themes of *Vandover and the Brute*. Again we see the absent mother, and the failure of the novel's chief female character to guide and uplift her man as the "man's woman" heroines

of later novels do.   These failed surrogate-mothers are almost intermixed;
Trina's name is a twisted version of that of Turner, Vandover's good woman,
and Trina was first named Bessie, the name of a minor character in *Vandover*,
in Norris's Harvard sketches.   Trina certainly does not covet money because
her "peasant blood ... hardy and penurious" gives her a hoarding instinct, any
more than she works at carving toy animals because "some worsted-leggined
wood-carver of the Tyrol" in her ancestry handed down the skill (*McTeague*
357, 358).   These few attempts at naturalistic heredity in *McTeague* are much
less convincing than Norris's picture of destructive ingrown sexuality.   Trina
is not simply a failed mother, but a non-mother, a reversal of the virtues of
archetypal motherhood that Blix and Lloyd portray, and her avarice is a
consistent part of this character.

The simplest illustration of this non-motherhood is that, like most
couples in these novels, Trina and her husband never have children.   There is
an amusing scene where McTeague is confused about Uncle Oelbermann
sending children's toys as a wedding present, but in the end, like the Jadwins,
the McTeagues are never even seen to wonder why three years of marriage
produce no fruit.   Trina does feed and look after her husband as his mother,
the nourishing cook, must have done, but she never raises him up as his
mother did.   Oscar Cargill fittingly uses one of Norris's favorite words to
describe McTeague's mother in lifting him from mining to dentistry through
her ambition and will: "No other force could have done it" (196).   (Perhaps no
force short of Gertrude Norris could have made Frank a disciplined writer,
either.)   But even Trina's few mediocre examples of the "making of men" that
women like Blix achieve—raising McTeague's material tastes, giving him the
golden tooth that symbolizes self-worth to him—soon fail.   When he loses his
job and she becomes miserly, there is "a general throwing off of the good
influence his wife had had over him in the days of their prosperity," until
McTeague sinks back into the anima-bereft indolence of the novel's first page.
"McTeague had lost his ambition.   He did not care to better his situation.   All
he wanted was a warm place to sleep and three good meals a day" (*McTeague*
475, 477).   And the tooth is sold to feed Trina's greed.

What does this female miser really represent?   Norris doesn't seem to
know, but most critics now agree that her money is a substitute for sex—or,
though this has not been said, maternal love.   Zerkow, too, marries Maria
through lust for gold (her probably-fictional gold dinner plates) rather than
physical lust, and she, naturally enough, joins the ranks of failed Norris
mothers when their child quickly dies, "a mere incident in their lives, a thing
that had come undesired and had gone unregretted" (431).   Trina, for her part,
becomes truly miserly only when her husband loses interest in her, supporting
Hochman's view that the true theme of *McTeague* is not greed but loss.   It is
her own "uncontrolled sexual responses" (now unfulfilled responses) that
make her wish for "control and self-sufficiency" through money (Hochman
69-70).   Michaels's link between Trina's masochism and her avarice—loving

submission for its own sake parallels loving money for its own sake (121)—is, though original, essentially the same point about money and desire that others have made. Norris underlines this heavily by showing Trina crying, "Ah, the dear money, the dear money ... I love you so!" (*McTeague* 478), burying her face in it, hugging it, and even (as practically every person ever to write about *McTeague* has quoted) sleeping with it.

A more subtle parallel appears in her own thoughts about her stinginess, "anyhow, I can't help it" (411), for McTeague's love for her is also described as involuntary. Love and money become the objects of a single desire—St. Paul's "root of all evil." This, and Trina's masochism, are Norris's ways of making procreation (or sex) look loathsome here, as is Vandover's reaction to childbirth in the earlier novel. There is no successful family in this novel, as there is not in *Vandover*; the Sieppes present some picture of normal domesticity, but an absurd and belittled one, and the two marriages that occur in the course of the story are grotesque mistakes. And Norris crowns this second novel of his post-disownment year with the creation of a woman who is a savage denial of motherhood.

Trina is no Hilma Tree. She is first described as small and pale (like Laura Jadwin after her) and almost anemic, although she does have the massive hair of a Norris heroine. She is also called a "not yet awakened" woman, "almost like a boy" (279). If McTeague, like Vandover, needs someone to replace his lost mother, he certainly doesn't find her in Trina. The most revealing passage in this context is when she weeps over her empty bag, after McTeague has stolen the money, "as other women weep over a dead baby's shoe" (510). For her own uterus is also doomed to be empty. Her only motherhood is Terrible Motherhood (Spangler calls this idea the "fatal woman"); for Jung describes the devouring archetype at one point in language the early Norris would approve of: she "leads the peoples into whoredom with her devilish temptations" (5:226). Trina is sex without generation, and McTeague's "agonizing void," the mother-longing which the voracious dentist shares with all men, cannot be fulfilled by marrying her.

So he kills her, and in return, nature as "fatal woman" kills him. Though Norris never consciously used the Garden of Eden as a metaphor even in *The Octopus*, an author so concerned with maternal images of nourishment and denied nourishment reflected in nature could hardly have avoided this reference. Death Valley, where McTeague dies of thirst, represents his punishing expulsion from the garden where all the world's fruits offer a respite from thirst and hunger. It is hardly surprising that Norris put the "death in the desert" into his first plot summary of *McTeague* at Harvard, rather than tacking it on in 1897 as some believe. The conflicts then raging in his mind are fully illustrated by this novel.

Clearly the belief stated in Leslie Fiedler's *Love and Death in the American Novel*, that child-bearing and the consummation of love are subjects missing from most American fiction (24), is especially true of Frank Norris.

Even in his later career, when he turned to romantic subjects (partly because he'd found romance in his life, and partly because he was surrendering to genre to finance that same romance), he was more concerned with females as mothers—but not physical mothers—than as lovers. One more relevant point made by Lynn is that the women chosen by Norris's heroes are surrogate mothers; they're tall and powerful because "the viewpoint from which they are described is that of a small boy looking at his mother." And this is why Norris's women are "teacher and guide" to their men, and why Norris cannot stand to contemplate sex between his heroes and heroines (184).

It isn't quite as simple as Lynn writes. The "teacher and guide" role is also connected, as shown before, to the genteel tradition of Norris's background, and physical love is far from unthinkable in the later novels. Wilbur sleeps beside Moran on the beach as noted, though he resists temptation. Condy contemplates Blix's fragrant neck, Annixter first wants Hilma only as a mistress, and Jadwin exclaims about Laura, "Charlie, upon my word, what a beautiful—what beautiful *hair* that girl has!" (*The Pit* 104)—presumably ready to say something more risque before he falls back on Norris's general sexual symbol. What *is* unthinkable is that any of these surrogate mothers, or rather surrogate Great Mothers, should become demeaned by the physical motherhood that appalls Vandover.

For this reason, the romances of the middle novels never end with the normal result of love in life, that normal result whose general absence Fiedler saw. Moran dies before any union with Wilbur can be consummated, *Blix* ends at the moment mutual love is discovered, and the couple in *A Man's Woman* marries, but Bennett sails off to confront the Terrible Mother again rather than having or raising children with Lloyd. Instead of becoming true mothers, the "men's women" in these books' titles play the role of mother to their men. (Moran, as seen in the last chapter, actually plays the role of father, so only the latter two books will be considered here.)

The escape-announcement nature of *Blix* has been described already. Norris presents Blix/Jeannette as the alternative to his own mother, who appears in the novel only as a few in-jokes, the foolish character K.D.B., and the invisible mother with whom Condy lives—not even in a real family home, but in a hotel. Hart thinks Condy's mother provides a "favorable influence" that the motherless Vandover doesn't have (*A Novelist in the Making* 24), but Condy is effectively motherless anyway. His mother is not even mentioned until four chapters of romance and ramblings with Blix have passed; and she is only mentioned once afterward, when "not to be at home" as noted before. Van's mother is actually a far greater presence in his novel than Condy's mother is in *Blix*. It is Travis Bessemer, herself motherless, who fills the gap, as her role of "mother" to Snooky and Howard shows—and to emphasize this, Norris opens the novel with scenes of the Bessemer family before we ever meet Condy. As Debra Munn writes, "It is disorganized and fidgety Howard who comes to mind later when Blix has to display remarkably appropriate psychology in her 'curing' of Condy" (55).

Thus, as we've seen, though French and other critics call both of *Blix*'s lead characters immature, only Condy is really childish. Yet Norris describes them both in his final scene as having lived only for the present as children do, though Blix was already reading her medical textbooks the day before. When they kiss and then face the sunset—a reversed symbol because this day marks the *end* of the West and the beginning of the "grim" working world of the East in their lives—Norris grants them both the awareness of all of life. "All the fine, virile, masculine energy of him was aroused and rampant. All her sweet, strong womanliness had been suddenly deepened and broadened. In fine, he had become a man, and she a woman" (275).

The letter offering Condy a job in New York, which even Norris realizes (calling it "a veritable god from the machine") is a ridiculous *deus ex machina* bestowed by the author to complete their happiness, is opened immediately afterward. And Condy and Blix's little games and roamings are over. Anyone who reads this book carefully can see that it is no more a celebration of immaturity than *A Man's Woman* is of brute strength. But Norris is still leaving something out; though he writes of work and of vague "possibilities of sorrow and trouble, of pleasure and of happiness" (277) in their future, he does not mention children or even marriage. Blix has made a man of Condy, but we are not told that she will ever make a father of him.

And we are not told that Lloyd will ever do the same for Ward Bennett. What she does is play Norris's two familiar roles for a romantic heroine: moral guide and non-physical mother. She is so much an example of the genteel tradition that unlike Hilma in reacting to Annixter's kissing her and to his first proposal, Lloyd is offended by Bennett merely thinking she loves him—though she does! "Tell me, how have I ever led you to believe that I cared for you?" she says coldly when he asks her to marry him (*A Man's Woman* 93); and when he reveals that Ferriss told him, she feels humiliated and demeaned, furious at Ferriss's "insult." This may be overplaying her proud role, but when she masters the sick Bennett later, Norris makes up very well for his absurd sexism in *McTeague* and *Moran*. Though he has, earlier in this novel as well, put in his usual scene of the woman enjoying being made "helpless" by masculine power, now he writes that "she could be masterful while he was weak" (204). The fact that Bennett finally *isn't* her master is the reason love returns—the opposite of why the women of the earlier novels fall in love.

But Norris complicates the issue further by his familiar passion for the powerful, benevolent mother-figure. It isn't the only thing happening here, as Lynn might claim, but is certainly part of it. "I don't want you to go. Don't leave me," says the feverish Bennett, his voice "quavering pitifully" (194) just as the once-forceful Moran's "deep voice trembled a little" after love conquered her (*Moran of the Lady Letty* 238). Of course Lloyd doesn't go, but like Blix, now that she has accepted the role of a sheltering mother she seems to have a child on her hands. "Ward, why will you be such a boy?" she exclaims in the next chapter, as her now-recovered patient acts surly and claims to be still weak and sick when she turns the conversation to exploring (*A Man's Woman* 196, 199). Norris later tells us that, like Annixter will after him, Bennett has become generous and kind; and Lloyd feels a protective "maternal instinct" which the author says now is always an element of woman's love. The Great Mother emerges: "She felt that she, not as herself individually, but as a woman, was not only stronger than Bennett, but in a manner older, more mature. She was conscious of depths in her nature far greater than in his, and also that she was capable of attaining heights of heroism, devotion, and sacrifice which he, for all his masculine force, could not only never reach, but could not even conceive of" (209). After a blunt statement that theirs is now almost a mother/son relationship, Norris hurries his novel to its nationalistic, America-cheering conclusion.

The position of *A Man's Woman* in the line of development of Norris's themes is so obvious that the novel's dismissal by critics is surprising. The other middle novels really are slight works, but this one, after we dig through the rubble of Norris's repetition and portentous capitalized ideas, reveals a perceptiveness about gender roles greater than that of the wheat novels. Turning next to *The Octopus*, we find Norris no longer merely exploring the nature of love—the previous novel has left him with nothing more to say—but combining his image of the ideal woman with, as seen before, the age-old realization of that image in Mother Nature.

There are more true mothers in *The Octopus* than in any other novel. Its three young male heroes, Annixter, Presley and Vanamee, have, like Ross Wilbur, no parents that we are ever told about; but the Derricks, the Dykes, the Hoovens, and the Trees are all complete or nearly complete families. Norris lampoons his own mother briefly in Mrs. Cedarquist, but he also creates a sentimental-song image of aged motherhood in Mrs. Dyke, "an old lady with a very gentle face, who wore a cap and a very old-fashioned gown with hoop skirts" (751). Her granddaughter Sidney is motherless, and Hilma miscarries, but weakness rather than total absence is the common fate of mothers here.

Now married, Norris could perhaps imagine ordinary, happy families better; but his old ambivalence never departed, and he destroyed or weakened most of these families in the course of the novel. Thus we have these final images, nearly as pathetic as that of Vandover's mother, of most of the mothers above: Annie Derrick, who shares the loss of two sons with Magnus, sad, apathetic and needing to work to support her dotard husband; Mrs. Dyke "worn out, abandoned and forgotten" after her son turns criminal, telling Presley she waits only for death (920); Mrs. Hooven dying "dumb, bewildered, stupid," unable to feed her young daughter or herself (1051). Even Angele Varian has to die in childbirth to produce the perfect daughter that renews Vanamee's love. The female God, the wheat, may punish S. Behrman, but somehow is not strong or willing enough to protect its fellow mothers in the novel beforehand.

The chief maternal figures in *The Octopus*, Annie and Hilma, offer a final illustration of Norris's contrasting of physical with archetypal mothers. Annie has much in common with Gertrude Norris—"an Easterner, and therefore effete," according to Richard Chase, who believes Norris dislikes the character (193), she is interested in literature and once taught writing, and is afraid of the vastness of the wheat-bearing valley. Norris first shows her reading Pater and holding her "over-fed" white cat, and says: "She was not made for the harshness of the world." She finds the "nakedness" of the ranch's earth "indecent," which shows her inability to appreciate, as the narrator does, its unashamed reproductive "elemental Female" role (*The Octopus* 623-4). It is difficult to picture her being pregnant with either of her own two children.

She does make some attempt to behave in the middle-novels mold of moral guide, opposing the other ranchers' efforts to make Magnus agree to the bribery scheme. But even this stance is presented as one of fear, "shrinking from the harshness of the world, striving, with vain hands, to draw her husband back with her" (719-20). And she fails anyway, since Magnus does join the corrupt scheme and is finally disgraced by its exposure. Even at this late stage of his career, Norris desperately condemns the "literature" side of his parental battle in the person of Annie: over and over she is described as weak and afraid of life's challenges, and the novel's view of humanity as an insect helpless against cold nature, usually ascribed to Norris, is actually presented as her thoughts.

The author does choose to show a gently maternal side to Annie when, during the rabbit drive, one frightened rabbit jumps into her lap for a moment. But even as a mother, her softness is unhelpful to her son Harran. Though Norris's notes focus on a contrast between Hilma and Angele Varian, the novel's real contrast in important female characters is between Hilma and Annie; and this is best shown in the one scene where they speak together, after the ditch ambush where Annixter is killed and Harran is mortally wounded. Annie whimpers and cries impotently, "Harrie, Harrie, oh, my son, my little boy" (the weak mother Mrs. Dyke also cried "my son, my son" after Dyke's crime); Hilma says angrily to her, "how *can* you—when Harran and your husband may be—may—are in danger," and remains strong at the scene of laid-out bodies, taking Annixter's hand and crying without sound (994, 998).

And for the rest of the novel she is presented as a tower of strength— just when she ceases to be a true potential mother. That night she has her miscarriage, and it is after this that the milky maiden of before fills the complete role of "man's woman." Her amply feminine figure has changed when Presley last sees her. "Hilma was dressed in black, the cut and fashion of the gown severe, almost monastic. All the little feminine and contradictory daintinesses were nowhere to be seen ... The one-time amplitude of her figure, the fullness of hip and shoulder, the great deep swell from waist to throat were gone ... Her neck was slender, the outline of her full lips and round chin was a little sharp; her arms, those wonderful, beautiful arms of hers, were a little shrunken" (1079).

What strange hormonal shifts brought about such an amazing transformation can only be guessed at. But what Norris is illustrating is clear: this is no longer a sexual woman, but a woman of the genteel tradition. Her childlike innocence of old—drinking from the creek and feeling it's "stupid to be grown up," going to sleep on her wedding night "with the directness of a little child, holding [Annixter's] hand in both her own" (835, 904)—is replaced by a cool maturity. Fittingly, Presley meets her at the Derricks' house just after Annie has "disappeared," and he doesn't want to see that weak-mother figure again after meeting Hilma. Instead he becomes, like Condy and Bennett before him, a man transfigured by a woman's goodness, resolving "to reshape his purposeless, wasted life with her nobility and purity and gentleness for his inspiration" (1080). In a Frank Norris novel, only a woman who has not borne children can fulfill this role.

This leads us to *The Pit*, which finishes Norris's career with the same final indecision about his mother as about his father. Laura never has children either, but she represents someone who did—Gertrude Norris.

Laura is many things besides a picture of Norris's mother: she is yet another genteel-tradition character, with her notorious "grand manner" and furious reaction when her first suitor, Landry, tries to kiss her; a second Presley in that the novel focuses on her unreliable perceptions of its events' meaning; and the opposite of Hilma, with "almost extreme slenderness" in which "the curves of her figure, the contour of her shoulders, the swell of hip and breast were all low," and a Trina-like paleness (1-2). She does have thick, abundant hair, like Trina and other potentially sexual Norris women, but her physique includes one clue to her inability to fulfill the middle-novel heroines' roles—"from head to foot one could discover no pronounced salience" (2). A person without a salient chin or jaw is a person without Frank Norris's stamp of approval.

Yet she is dignified and beautiful, and though her self-centered ennui becomes tiresome, we can understand this selfishness via Norris's own knowledge of his mother's New England upbringing. His lack of complete respect for the character is compensated throughout by his sympathy for her, just as we would expect. He knows why she feels bored and lonely, with her businessman husband and her oversized house, and he knows why Corthell touches a space within her spirit that Jadwin cannot find.

Critics are divided on *The Pit*. Warren French sees it as a novel whose "characters and events are ... drawn from observation rather than myth," and thus finally shows some self-analysis (116); French seems to have missed the self-analysis in *Vandover* at least, but *The Pit* certainly has it, and this critic is right in seeing the Laura plot as more important than the "pit" scenes which other readers wished to see emphasized. One such earlier critic, Ernest Marchand, thought of Laura as an "idle egoistic woman" and the love story as weakening the "epic theme," since the wheat no longer dominates (83, 86). But Norris had already made his presentation of the Great Mother; it couldn't be repeated in a novel that was of personal rather than epic size. Passages about the wheat's power here seem like clashing, awkwardly-inserted notes. This is not the world of Hilma, but of Annie, and accurate as the "idle egoistic" description of Laura may be, it's right that she, not the wheat or the mock-mythic Jadwin, should dominate this novel.

But there *is* an undercurrent common to the wheat novels, as Charles Hoffman saw when he wrote that the "regenerative power of love" appears in both (514). Hoffman, one of the 1950s critics who first called Norris a moralist rather than a naturalist, felt that Jadwin is morally redeemed despite the hellish force-symbol of the pit itself—which is also, though no one seems to have stated the obvious, another Terrible Mother's womb sucking men back in. It is this symbol, not that of the nourishing wheat, that probably remains with readers of *The Pit*. This is because Norris was not sure how to present either womanhood or Laura here, moving toward and then away from making her another "man's woman." For example, he wrote of her thinking just after her marriage that "love, the supreme triumph of a woman's life, was less a victory than a capitulation" (*The Pit* 194), but not long afterward she is being selfish and materialistic again. Certainly Norris saw Laura as the center of the novel, but his biographer tells us that he found writing a book with this focus (not surprisingly) difficult; unlike with *The Octopus*, he didn't enjoy the work and revised it often (Walker 291).

The dilemma is finally solved somewhat by Norris's putting the self-sacrificing moral guide theme into the mouth of a character other than Laura: her sister Page (who is until then only a humble "page" in Laura's court of admirers). Her romance with Landry is a smaller, less serious version of the main story, but ends more happily. And even if Norris's anti-feminist view, as in *A Man's Woman*, of the ideal woman as one who sits silently and backs up her husband is seen as disquieting, it is a relief after hundreds of pages of Laura's actress histrionics—"I only want to be loved for my own sake, and not—and not—when I want to be, oh, loved—loved—loved" (164), or "I will be happy. I will, I will, I will! ... I hate you; I hate you all. I hate this house, I hate this life. You are all killing me" (289)—to hear Page lecture to her that a woman should help and support her man, right or wrong.

Of course, Gertrude Norris did want to be loved, just as her son did; and perhaps he also sensed in childhood that she hated her rich facade of a house and a life. Laura is, as a few critics have said, more real than most other Norris characters, and this is understandable considering her model. When Norris returns once more to his familiar double-personality idea, here writing that one Laura is a quiet housewife, the other a frustrated actress (one is Jadwin's, the other Corthell's, though he doesn't write that) (238), it resonates more than at any other time. The roots of his own dialectic were in the dialectic suffered by his mother.

5

Conclusion

TOWARD the end of *The Novels of Frank Norris,* Donald Pizer sums up this author by writing that his view of a woman's role as "self-sacrificing helpmate to a man of action" is so weak that it weakens all of his novels that focus on it, rather than those of which it is only a part (178). This is true if we share the most familiar critical opinion of Frank Norris: that *McTeague* and *The Octopus,* and perhaps *Vandover and the Brute,* are the novels to remember him by, but *The Pit* and especially the middle novels would be forgotten without these better works to keep his reputation alight. Perhaps they would be forgotten, but masculine novels full of healthy brutality have tended to occupy a higher spot in the canon than novels about love and homemaking. This is what Leslie Fiedler did not see: that it's the American novels critics *tell* us are great, like *Moby Dick* and *Huckleberry Finn,* that are so empty of loving female influence. Certainly these books are both superb, as is *The Octopus* in its own way; but we should not dismiss novels by Norris or anyone else that present genteel romance "purified by feminine idealism" (George Johnson's comment on the change in Bennett) without asking ourselves whether the seeming triviality of this subject matter is the reason we're dismissing them. Pizer was right to also conclude that Norris is less a great novelist than a writer whose themes and imagination are strong enough to still interest us (*The Novels of Frank Norris* 179), but that strength is not absent from the less red-blooded works.

Norris focused on gender relationships because the pull of two genders (or what they seemed to represent) was such a central aspect of his psyche. This is why Carl Jung, with his theory of the underlying image of mother and father for each of us, comes to mind here. Anima and animus, Yin and Yang, Eros and Logos, the body-v.-spirit debate of the 19th century—all of these are expressions of a duality to which Norris could never quite find a solution. When he wrote *McTeague,* he had no answer, and only anti-mother images like the miserly Trina and the waterless Death Valley; but by the time of *The Octopus,* he sought the image of the Great Mother as a unifier, both of the novel's conflicts and of his personal Yes and No. This climaxed in the "larger view" conclusion which critics have derided as "ridiculous," making even S. Behrman a force for good (Hicks 173), and "contrary to all one has witnessed in the book" (Ziff 268). Such views are understandable when, after displaying so much suffering and death, the author asserts that the universe is a benign, just place. But the ending is not a contrary one at all, for the Mother, seen especially in the wheat and Hilma, casts her huge, benevolent gaze over the entire novel.

Norris felt the mother-longing of which Jung wrote, not because his own mother fulfilled his needs so well, but because she didn't fulfill them. But as he grew beyond the conflicts of his youth, in which he worked to please her but then felt guilty about not pleasing his father, he must have felt some sense of reconciliation. He was, after all, now a success at the profession she had chosen for him. And his discovery of love, as celebrated in *Blix*, probably helped against the sense of instability and disorder which Barbara Hochman believed was his chief theme. Even Ahnebrink, who saw Norris as a naturalist, wrote: "Sex became a moral and ennobling emotion in *The Octopus* and *The Pit*. The naturalistic psychology of desire gave way to a moralistic psychology of will" (212).

Norris's attempt to follow a consciously scientific theory, naturalistic determinism, at the same time as he revealed a genteel viewpoint drawn from religion, reminds us of Jung's points about rationalist materialism v. mysticism (recognition of the unconscious). Jung respected religion as a preserver of myth, but himself saw sex as "moral and ennobling" rather than as Calvinistic sin; he even found it something of an answer to the problem of fulfilling parentally-inspired roles—exactly the problem Norris had. However, though his view of parental archetypes—the nourishing and devouring mother, the punishing superego of the father—lends itself well to the arguments here, Jung's lifetime of analyzing mythology and comparative religion leads to much relevant material beyond what has already been cited. For example, he writes of the Aztec corn-god, the Chinese custom of emperors ploughing a furrow, and the old European idea of kings' "marriage with the land," which led one king to be killed because of a failure of crops (Jung 5:357), all of which can be connected to the theme of *The Octopus*. There is clearly even more that could be said to connect Jung with Norris.

Yet even without this psychological guide, we cannot miss the concern with duality that characterizes the Norris who straddled the 19th and 20th centuries, East and West, "life" and "literature." It is appropriate that a battle of contrasting literary categories, Romance and Realism—finally portrayed by Norris as Corthell v. the Silas Lapham-like Jadwin—should have gone on during his lifetime, and that he should have claimed loyalty to both sides at once. His wish to be "in-dividual" can be seen in his attempt to create what H. Willard Reninger called "romantic-reality." He even tried to see public taste in novels as low and needing to be guided, and yet the correct arbiter of a work's value at the same time. Thus this writer often identified with American naturalism personified the "divided stream" which Charles Child Walcutt saw in that movement.

But his dialectic was always a personal battle as well. He tried to transcend his own "dvandva" caused by the contrasting personalities of Frank

(Sr.) and Gertrude Norris, which he characterized in writing in many ways, such as his doctrine of thinking-v.-feeling. He was always concerned with finding a way to fulfill both the maternally and paternally-centered sides of himself, and thus created male characters like Ward Bennett who needed feminine purifying, and female characters like Moran who were as strong as men. This conflict was not resolved until he married, an act which gave him the independence Franklin Walker felt he needed "to realize his greatest powers" (150)—or perhaps more correctly, to write his most mature novels. For the tormented pages of *Vandover and the Brute* and *McTeague* do have great power, but their single-minded views of life, and especially of sex, make them inferior to the wheat novels.

It is in fact the critical focus on *McTeague*, and on the less gender-centered aspects of *The Octopus*, that has often led to misguided negative opinions of Frank Norris. From the time Howells called *McTeague* a "case in point" to encourage young writers to attempt less European-influenced fiction, the story of the brutal dentist has been regarded as Norris's chief legacy, because it helped implant realism in America. But critics of 30-40 years ago who began to call Norris romantic and humanist were closer to the truth; and this view, and the aspects of the writer explored in more recent years, show a necessity to examine his later works more closely. *A Man's Woman* in particular needs a less prejudiced reading.

The "man's woman" theme itself probably meant more to Norris by the end of his life than his earlier atavism theme. Norris believed this simple, innocent exchange in *Blix*—"'Condy, *is* there anything in the world better or finer than a strong man?' 'Not unless it is a good woman, Blix'" (161)—and spent the rest of his career trying to dramatize it. Blix's "fine sweet feminine strength" (173), which not only makes Condy more determined and masculine but even finally lowers his voice; Lloyd's maternal devotion and "strong, womanly encouragement" (*A Man's Woman* 237) that sends Bennett back out exploring; Hilma telling Annixter, "My husband is such a *good* man ... Just because you love me true" (*The Octopus* 923); Page's final lecture to her older sister in *The Pit*—all these scenes and phrases show the firm rooting of this theme in the later novels.

But a theme which persisted throughout Norris's career, bigness, may represent him best. It unites both his early and late fiction, for both McTeague and Presley find their chief comfort in immensity and the "larger view" offered by Mother Nature. This finally led to a greater humanism as well, as Norris turned away from the imperialistic pursuits of the days when he had been trying to please his father's image, and accepted success in the once mother-guided profession which now served to support his wife and daughter. Marchand wrote that "Norris groped his way from the notion of the primordial struggle for existence to the concept of a common social enterprise in which individual self-assertion must yield to the general good" (173). We've seen that the author was hardly such a socialist in *The Octopus*, but he did in the end become more tolerant of those who had not participated in the Anglo-Saxon march, and was "groping" (exactly the right word) toward reconciling his father's Alger-myth conservatism with his own vague ideas about exalting the People and fighting injustice.

This "big" view can be seen in a passage he wrote late in life, remarkable words from the pen of one who had seemed so racist. "Will it not go on, this epic of civilization, this destiny of the races, until at last and at the ultimate end of all, we who now arrogantly boast ourselves as Americans, supreme in conquest, whether of battle-ship or of bridge-building, may realize that the true patriotism is the brotherhood of man and know that the whole world is our nation and simple humanity our countrymen?" ("The Frontier Gone at Last," *Frank Norris: Novels and Essays* 1189-90). Thus this man who so well represented two centuries finally voiced not only the Rooseveltian delight in conquest which characterized his own time, but the Wilsonian internationalist idealism which would follow his death.

Returning to the first points made in this study of Frank Norris, we can now see clearly why George Johnson wrote of his attempts to resolve ambiguities. Where Johnson was wrong was in saying these attempts caused the flaws in Norris's novels—in fact, they are a main source of the novels' strengths. But this critic offers us an excellent summary of Norris when he writes, "The ultimate West was the justificiation of his ostensible optimism, the inevitability of the sunset the basis for despair" ("The Frontier Behind Frank Norris's *McTeague*" 103).

The Anglo-Saxon in Norris's essays always marches West, and the dead Moran sails away on a boat with "bowsprit held due west ... out to the world of romance" (*Moran of the Lady Letty* 291). But Norris finally admitted the inevitability, not exactly of the sunset, but of the sunset's end—the loss of romance, the lessening that Carl Jung saw in modern life of the unconscious or feminine side of our psyches. The image we finally see, again, is that of the lovers in *Blix* with "their backs forever turned to the sunset" (278) and facing the grim, masculine East. It is one more image, like McTeague in the desert or *Moran*'s hero and heroine leaving their prehistoric beach, of a loss of Eden—for Milton, too, following the Bible's suggestion, sends his exiles East, so that they, "looking back, all the eastern side beheld/of Paradise, so late their happy seat/waved over by that flaming brand" (303)—a flame just like that in *Blix*'s sunset.

And as in Norris's novel, there is a hopeful future for Milton's Adam and Eve—"The world was all before them, where to choose/Their place of rest, and Providence their guide" (303)—but no longer an innocent, womb-enclosed one. What Jung calls "rebirth in the Western Sea" (5:331)—immortality by the grace of the Great Mother—is not offered to any of these characters, though Frank Norris himself wished for it most of all.

Works Cited

Works by Norris

Frank Norris: Novels and Essays. Contents: *Vandover and the Brute, McTeague, The Octopus* and literary essays. Ed. and with notes by Donald Pizer. New York: Library of America, 1986. (Page citations from *Vandover and the Brute* are from this book.)

A Man's Woman. Vol. 6 of the *Complete Edition of Frank Norris.* Garden City, NY: Doubleday, 1928.

Moran of the Lady Letty: A Story of Adventure off the California Coast. New York: AMS Press, 1971.

A Novelist in the Making. Contents: **Vandover and the Brute, Blix** and student themes. Ed. and with an introduction by James D. Hart. Cambridge: Harvard U. Press, 1970.

The Pit: A Story of Chicago. Vol. 9 of the *Complete Edition.* Foreword by Juliet Wilbur Tompkins.

Works by Others

Ahnebrink, Lars. *The Beginnings of Naturalism in American Fiction.* New York: Russell & Russell, Inc., 1961.

Bixler, Paul H. "Frank Norris's Literary Reputation." *American Literature* 6:2 (May 1934): 109-21.

Brooks, Van Wyck. *The Confident Years: 1885-1915.* New York: Dutton, 1955.

Cargill, Oscar. *Intellectual America: Ideas on the March.* New York: Macmillan, 1941.

Chase, Richard. *The American Novel and Its Tradition.* Baltimore: Johns Hopkins U., 1957.

Clayre, Alisdair. *The Heart of the Dragon.* London: Collins/Harvill, 1984.

Cooper, Frederic Taber. *Some American Story Tellers.* London: Grant Richards Ltd., 1912.

Cooperman, Stanley. "Frank Norris and the Werewolf of Guilt." *Modern Language Quarterly* 20:3 (Sep. 1959): 252-8.

Dillingham, William B. "Frank Norris and the Genteel Tradition." *Tennessee Studies in Literature* 5 (1960): 15-24.

---. *Frank Norris: Instinct and Art.* Lincoln, NE: U. of Nebraska Press, 1969.

Fenton, John Y. et al. *Religions of Asia.* 2nd ed. New York: St. Martin's Press, 1988.

Fiedler, Leslie A. *Love and Death in the American Novel.* New York: Stein & Day, 1966.

Freedman, William. "Oral Passivity and Oral Sadism in Norris's *McTeague.*" *Literature and Psychology* 30:2 (1980): 52-61.

French, Warren. *Frank Norris.* New Haven: College and University Press, 1962.

Geismar, Maxwell. *Rebels and Ancestors: The American Novel 1890-1915.* Boston: Houghton Mifflin, 1953.

Gohdes, Clarence. "The Facts of Life v. Pleasant Reading." In Arthur Hobson Quinn, ed., *The Literature of the American People.* New York: Appleton-Century-Crofts, 1951. 737-62.

Graham, Don. *The Fiction of Frank Norris: The Aesthetic Context.* Columbia, MO: U. of Missouri Press, 1978.

Hicks, Granville. *The Great Tradition: An Interpretation of American Literature Since the Civil War.* New York: Macmillan, 1935.

Hochman, Barbara. *The Art of Frank Norris, Storyteller.* Columbia, MO: U. of Missouri Press, 1988.

Hoffman, Charles G. "Norris and the Responsibility of the Novelist." *South Atlantic Quarterly* 54:4 (Oct. 1955): 508-15.

Horton, Rod W., and Herbert W. Edwards. *Backgrounds of American Literary Thought.* Englewood Cliffs, NJ: Prentice-Hall, 1974.

Howells, W. D. "Frank Norris." *North American Review* 175 (Nov. 1902): 769-78.

Johnson, George W. "Frank Norris and Romance." *American Literature* 33:1 (Mar. 1961): 52-63.

---. "The Frontier Behind Frank Norris's *McTeague.*" *Huntington Library Quarterly* 26:1 (1962): 91-104.

Jung, C. G. *The Collected Works.* Trans. by R.F.C. Hull. London: Routledge & Kegan Paul, 1956. 20 Vols.

Katz, Joseph. "Eroticism in American Literary Realism." *Studies in American Fiction* 5:1 (Spring 1977): 35-50.

Kazin, Alfred. *On Native Grounds: An Interpretation of Modern American Literature.* New York: Harcourt, Brace, 1942.

Love, Glen A. "Frank Norris's Western Metropolitans." *Western American Literature* 11:1 (Spring 1976): 3-22.

Lutwack, Leonard. *Heroic Fiction: The Epic Tradition and American Novels of the 20th Century.* Carbondale, IL: Southern Illinois U. Press, 1971.

Lynn, Kenneth S. *The Dream of Success: A Study of the Modern American Imagination.* Boston: Little, Brown, 1955.

Marchand, Ernest. *Frank Norris: A Study.* New York: Octagon Books, 1971.

Marcosson, Isaac F. *Adventures in Interviewing.* New York: John Lane, 1919.

Martin, Jay. *Harvests of Change: American Literature 1865-1914.* Englewood Cliffs, NJ: Prentice-Hall, 1967.

McElrath. Joseph R., Jr. "The Erratic Design of Frank Norris's *Moran of the Lady Letty.*" *American Literary Realism 1870-1910* 10:2 (Spring 1977): 114-24.

---. "Frank Norris's *Vandover and the Brute*: Narrative Technique and the Socio-Critical Viewpoint." *Studies in American Fiction* 4:1 (Spring 1976): 27-43.

Michaels, Walter Benn. *The Gold Standard and the Logic of Naturalism: American Literature at the Turn of the Century.* Berkeley, CA: U. of California Press, 1987.

Milton, John. Excerpts from *Paradise Lost.* In Helen Gardner, ed., *The New Oxford Book of English Verse.* Oxford: Clarendon Press, 1972.

Mitchell, Lee Clark. *Determined Fictions: American Literary Naturalism.* New York: Columbia U. Press, 1989.

Munn, Debra D. "The Revision of Frank Norris's *Blix.*" *Resources for American Literary Study* 10:1 (Spring 1980): 47-55,

Pizer, Donald. "The Masculine-Feminine Ethic in Frank Norris's Popular Novels." *Texas Studies in Literature & Language* 6:1 (Spring 1964): 84-91.

---. *The Novels of Frank Norris.* New York: Haskell House, 1973.

---. *Realism and Naturalism in 19th-Century American Literature.* Carbondale, IL: Southern Illinois U. Press, 1966.

---. "Romantic Individualism in Garland. Norris and Crane." *American Quarterly* 10:4 (Winter 1958): 463-75.

Reninger. H. Willard. "Norris Explains *The Octopus*: A Correlation of his Theory and Practice." *American Literature* 12 (1940): 218-27.

Sherwood. John C. "Norris and the *Jeannette.*" *Philological Quarterly* 37:2 (Apr. 1958): 245-52.

Smrz, Vladimir. *American Economic Problems as Reflected in the Work of Frank Norris.* Thesis, Charles University, Prague (no date).

Spangler, George M. "The Structure of *McTeague.*" *English Studies* 59:1 (Feb. 1978): 48-56.

Stevens, Anthony. *Archetypes: Jung and the Ethologists.* London: Routledge & Kegan Paul, 1982.

Walcutt, Charles Child. *American Literary Naturalism, A Divided Stream.* Minneapolis: U. of Minnesota Press, 1956.

Walker, Franklin. *Frank Norris: A Biography.* New York: Russell & Russell, 1963.

Ziff, Larzer. *The American 1890s: Life and Times of a Lost Generation.* Lincoln, NE: U. of Nebraska Press, 1966.

Index

Ahnebrink, Lars, 14, 21, 22, 32, 39, 42, 45, 46, 61, 105, 121
Alger, Horatio, 6, 21, 25, 40
America in Norris's time, 5, 33, 43
  imperialism, 5, 9, 41
  Social Darwinism, 6, 23, 39, 80
Art v. commerce, 28, 68, 69, 77
  money symbolism, 68, 112-3
Augustine, St., 60

Barrie, *Peter Pan,* 4
Bierce, Ambrose, 21, 51
Bixler, Paul, 21, 98
Black, Jeannette (wife), 4, 13-4, 33, 34, 37, 52, 53, 59, 99, 103, 105, 107, 109
Blake, William, 98
Brooks, Van Wyck, 22

Cargill, Oscar, 61, 64, 94, 106, 112
Chase, Richard, 4, 35, 50, 72, 88, 117
Christian determinism, 10
Cooper, Frederic Taber, 20, 22, 51, 108
Cooper, James Fenimore, 5, 43, 44
Cooperman, Stanley, 10, 22, 47, 73, 111
Crane, Stephen, 1, 3, 4, 21, 22, 31, 43, 51

Darwin, Charles, 6, 55
Davis, Richard Harding, 44
Determinism in naturalism, 4
Dialectic (search for unity), 1, 10, 14, 35, 37, 51-2, 56, 59, 98-9, 110, 120-1
  "romantic-reality," 51, 121
Dickens, Charles, 1, 26, 43, 44, 45

Dillingham, William B., 6, 9, 16, 22, 23, 30, 41, 50, 69, 71, 107
Dreiser, Theodore, 3, 45, 50
  Norris champions *Sister Carrie,* 34, 45
Dvandva and nirdvandva, 59, 74, 98, 110, 122

"Earth Mother," 15
Eden image, 60, 67, 96, 113, 123
Emerson, Ralph, 10, 11, 22, 41, 54, 60, 100
Europe, dialectic with America, 4

Father as archetype, 57-8, 59, 63, 75, 82, 86, 100
Father images in novels, 15, 60, 62, 75-93, 94
Faulkner, William, 15
Fiedler, Leslie, 113-4, 120
Freedman, William, 24, 68, 79, 95
French, Warren, 7, 8, 10, 21, 22, 25, 29, 41, 45, 66, 67, 72, 77, 91-2, 96, 115, 118
Freud, Sigmund, 24, 56, 57, 63, 77, 80

Gates, Lewis, 12, 30, 44, 45 ,72
Geismar, Maxwell, 7, 21, 42, 58, 74, 77, 84
"Genteel Tradition," 6, 15-6, 18, 20, 47, 108, 114, 115, 118
Goethe, *Faust,* 94
Gohdes, Clarence, 39, 43-4
Graham, Don, 8, 23, 25, 46, 72, 91, 92, 100, 104, 105

Hart, James, 31, 44, 78, 108, 114
Hemingway, Ernest, 94

Hicks, Granville, 20, 21, 38, 92-3,
    120
Hochman, Barbara, 2, 23, 46, 70-1,
    76, 78, 99, 111, 112
Hodgson, "Captain Jack," 46, 80,
    85
Hoffman, Charles, 21, 119
Homer, 8, 44
Homosexuality, 101
Howells, William Dean, 3, 20, 48,
    52, 53, 95, 122
Huntington, Collis (model for
    Shelgrim), 31, 33, 37-8

Ibsen, Henrik, 42

James, Henry, 72
Johnson, George, 1, 6, 8, 12, 22,
    35, 51, 62, 71, 86, 95, 120, 123
Jung, Carl, 3, 6, 35, 54-7, 58, 59,
    61, 63, 64, 65, 68, 79, 94-5, 96,
    97, 98-9, 100-1, 102, 103, 107,
    109, 110, 113, 120, 121, 123
    "animus and anima"
        concept, 3, 55, 65, 120
    death-wish and
        regression theme, 95-6,
        101, 102
    "Great Mother"
        archetype, 3, 14, 32, 52, 55-6,
        57, 62, 68, 79, 94-5, 98-100,
        102, 103, 110, 111, 116,
        119, 120-1, 123
    "individuation" theme,
        57, 59
    "Terrible Mother," 35, 55, 95,
        97-8, 100, 102, 105, 113, 114,
        119
    Tribal-army bonding, 58, 68
    Unconscious (anima), 55, 56,
        94, 98-9, 123

Katz, Joseph, 74
Kazin, Alfred, 43, 60, 91
Keats, John, 23
Kipling, Rudyard, 9, 21, 24, 32,
    41, 53

Le Conte, Joseph, 6, 7, 10, 30, 41
Leiter, Joseph (model for Jadwin),
    46
Lewis, Sinclair, 25
Libido, 59, 63, 64, 83, 100
Lincoln, Abraham, 91
Locke, John, 55
Lombroso, Cesare, 41, 54
London, Jack, 1, 21, 22, 41, 51, 52,
    72, 81, 94
Longfellow, Henry Wadsworth ,
    101
Love, Glen A., 23, 37, 66, 67, 79,
    88
Lutwack, Leonard, 44, 61, 88
Lynn, Kenneth, 6, 12, 13, 16, 21-2,
    23, 27, 30, 32, 38, 41, 60, 68, 69,
    74, 81, 83, 88, 104, 110, 114, 115

Marchand, Ernest, 21, 38, 44, 46,
    47, 49, 63, 89, 91, 94, 105, 119,
    122
Marcosson, Isaac, 4, 20, 34, 46
Martin, Jay, 23, 39, 62, 68, 85
McElrath, Joseph, 3, 23-4, 80-1
McKinley, William, 9, 40
Melville, *Moby Dick,* 120
Michaels, Walter Benn, 24, 68,
    111, 113
Milton, John, 123
Mitchell, Lee, 49
Moody, Dwight, 26, 69
Mother, 57 (see Jung, Great
    Mother and Terrible Mother)
    Sea as symbol, 32, 65, 97, 101,
    104

Mother complex, 100-1, 107
Mothers (physical) in novels, 15, 102, 109, 110-9
Munn, Debra, 23, 70, 106, 107, 109, 114

Naturalism (doctrine), 71
  Body-soul theme, 10, 47
  Differences in Europe and America, 10, 39, 45, 118
Nature as feminine symbol, 11, 48, 55-6, 62, 82, 95, 96-8, 99-100, 113, 116
Newton, Isaac, 55, 98
Nietzsche, Friedrich, 1, 61
Norris, Charles, 12, 25, 26, 27-8, 32, 34, 104
Norris, Frank Sr., 1, 6, 12, 17, 25-8, 30, 57-8, 59, 69, 71, 85, 86, 88, 90, 104, 122
  Divorce and disowning, 1, 12, 13, 27, 30, 38, 58, 66, 75, 110
Norris, Frank Jr.:
Aesthetic awareness, 23, 104-5
Anti-city, 39, 67-8, 90, 95
Anti-intellectualism, 11, 13, 23
Berkeley years, 12, 13, 28, 29-30, 69, 105
Classism, 29, 42
Criticism of society, 33, 104, 109
Defined as moralist, 21, 22, 40, 119
Defined as naturalist by critics, 3, 4, 19-20, 21, 46, 121
Engine symbolism, 49-50, 64, 99
Football fan, 7, 13, 27, 28, 30, 36
God-images in the novels, 60-1, 64, 76, 77, 89, 95, 100
Harvard writing studies, 12, 21, 27, 31, 32, 44, 69, 111, 112, 113, 121
Increase in literary reputation, 23
Male names for female characters, 58-9

Norris, Frank Jr. contd.
Naivete and youthfulness, 4, 20, 47, 59, 65-6
Painting career attempt, 1, 23, 26, 27-8, 48-9, 56, 69, 103
Patriotism, 20, 35-6
Prudishness and moralizing, 18
Racism, 5, 41-2, 90
  Anglo-Saxon superiority idea, 8, 15, 21, 35, 37, 40-1, 58, 123
  Anti-Semitism, 41-2
San Francisco importance, 5, 31-2
San Francisco *Wave* correspondent, 13, 24, 31, 45
Victorianism, 7
War correspondent, Norris as, 2, 7, 13, 30-1, 34, 41, 46, 48, 66, 69, 71, 80, 86
Writer's block period, 32-3, 69
Themes in Norris's works:
Artist as weak self-image, 2, 14, 16-7, 32, 50, 71, 72, 105
"Brute," 6, 7, 8, 18, 47, 56,76, 96
Businessman as hero, 2, 15, 28, 35-7, 66, 68
California significance, 1
Clothes as motif, 72-3, 81, 83
"Enemy," 62, 64, 85-6, 87, 97-8, 99, 101, 102
"Force," 15, 49, 63-5, 73, 89, 91-2
Gambling as vice, 36, 53, 63, 88, 90-1, 98-100, 109
"Life" v. "literature," 2, 17, 50, 70-1, 74, 102-3
Love, 4-5, 16, 103, 107-8, 109, 115-6
"Man's woman," 1, 2, 6, 16, 18-9, 53, 87, 106-7, 109, 112, 114, 117-8, 119, 122
Masculine-feminine struggle, 4, 24
New York symbolism, 1
"Second self," 13, 59, 93, 119

Norris, Themes contd.
Sex as sin/brutality, 4-5, 7, 8-9, 11,
    17-8, 57, 103, 108, 109, 110-1,
    113
"Superman," 61-2, 78, 86, 89
Violence, 1, 5, 8, 9, 13, 71, 80, 84
West as Romance, 2, 42-3, 45-6,
    51, 115, 123
Wheat, 10, 14, 50, 55-6, 60, 64-5,
    72, 94-5, 97, 100, 102, 103, 116-
    7, 119, 121
Women as redeemer, 9, 18-9, 108,
    120
Women as strong and masculine,
    6, 16, 32, 94, 105-7, 122
Works by Norris:
"Accuracy v. Truth," 51
Blix, 2, 5, 6, 8, 9, 13, 14, 16, 18,
    19, 20, 23, 31, 32, 33, 35, 37, 42,
    44, 46-7, 48, 51, 52-3, 63, 67, 69,
    70, 80, 84-5, 96, 97, 100, 102-3,
    104, 105-7, 108-9, 114-5, 121,
    122, 123
"A Case for Lombroso," 41
"A Deal in Wheat," 24
"Dying Fires," 2, 32
"Fiction Is Selection," 51
"The Frontier Gone at Last," 15,
    37, 42
A Man's Woman, 2, 5, 6, 9, 10, 11,
    12, 13, 14, 16, 18, 19, 20, 22, 33,
    35-6, 42, 46, 47, 48, 50, 51, 53,
    56, 59, 61, 62-3, 64, 66, 67, 70,
    74, 80, 85-8, 93, 95, 96, 97-8,
    102, 103, 104-5, 106-7, 109, 114,
    115, 119, 122
McTeague, 1, 3, 4-5, 7, 8, 9, 10,
    11, 14, 16, 17-8, 20, 22, 24, 26,
    31, 32, 33, 39-40, 41, 42, 44-5,
    46, 47, 49, 50, 51, 64, 65, 67, 68,
    69, 71, 75, 76, 78-80, 87, 95-6,
    97-8, 103, 104, 107-8, 110, 113,
    115, 120, 122

Norris, Works contd.
Moran of the Lady Letty, 2, 4, 5,
    6, 7, 8, 9, 10, 11, 13, 14, 16, 17,
    18, 19, 23-4, 26, 29, 31, 32, 33,
    35, 40, 44, 46, 47, 50, 51, 58-9,
    65, 66, 67, 70, 72-3, 75, 80-5, 86,
    87, 97-8, 101, 102, 103, 104, 105,
    108, 114, 115, 123
"The Novel with a Purpose," 38
"Novelists of the Future," 70
The Octopus, 1, 5, 8, 9, 11, 14-5,
    16, 17, 18, 19, 20, 22, 26, 29, 31,
    32, 33, 34, 35, 37-8, 39, 40, 41,
    42-3, 44, 46, 47, 48, 49, 50, 51,
    52, 55-6, 59, 60, 61-2, 63, 64, 67-
    8, 69, 72, 73, 74, 75, 76, 83, 84,
    85, 88-90, 94, 97, 98, 99, 105,
    108, 113, 116-8, 119, 120, 121,
    122, 123
The Pit, 5, 8, 13, 14, 16, 18, 25-6,
    27, 29, 31, 33-4, 35, 36, 41, 42,
    47, 48, 49, 51, 53, 56, 57-8, 60,
    62, 64, 65, 66, 69, 71-5, 79, 90-3,
    94-5, 100, 105, 108, 114, 118-9,
    120, 121, 122
    Jadwins as Norris's parents, 16,
        25-6, 32, 74-5, 90, 118-9
"A Plea for Romantic Fiction," 51-
    2
*The Responsibilities of the
    Novelist*, 24, 51, 70
"The Responsibilities of the
    Novelist," 29, 69-71, 80
"Story-tellers v. Novelists," 71
"This Animal of a Buldy Jones," 28
"The True Reward of the Novelist,"
    69, 70
Vandover and the Brute, 3, 4-5, 8,
    10, 11, 12, 14, 15, 16, 17, 18, 21,
    23, 27, 28, 30, 31, 32, 40, 42, 44,
    45, 47, 48, 49, 51, 59, 60, 63, 64,
    67, 68, 69, 72, 73, 75-9, 80, 81,
    90, 96, 100, 101-2, 104, 105, 107,
    110-2, 113, 114, 118, 120, 122

Norris, Works contd.
The Wolf (unwritten), 34, 93
Yvernelle, 12, 26, 28, 36, 72
"Zola as a Romantic Writer," 47-8
Norris, Gertrude, 1, 4, 6, 12, 25,
  26-8, 30, 37, 52, 59, 85, 92, 94,
  102, 103-4, 105, 108, 110, 112,
  117, 118, 119, 122
    New England significance in
      life, 13, 25, 32, 118
Norris, Jeannette (daughter), 34,
  58
Norris, Lester, 26, 27

O'Neill, Eugene, 27

Paris, influence on Norris, 1, 4, 16,
  27-8, 34, 43
Pater, Walter, 117
Pizer, Donald, 2, 7, 8, 14, 16, 19,
  22, 23, 28, 37, 38, 39, 41, 45, 48,
  56, 60, 64, 70, 71, 86, 94, 95,
  100, 120
Poe, Edgar Allan, 101
Porter, Cole, 23

Realism, 2, 3, 20, 48, 50-2, 104,
  121, 122
Reninger, H. Willard, 51, 52, 121
Richard the Lion-Hearted, 15, 36,
  58
Rockwell, Norman, 91
Romanticism, 3, 48, 50-2, 69, 88,
  121
    Norris romantic
      individualism, 39
Roosevelt, Theodore, 7, 21, 39, 41,
  123
"Rta" (Hindu), 63-4, 80, 83, 98

Scott, Sir Walter, 26, 30, 43
Sherwood, James C., 22, 46, 50
Sinclair, Upton, 35
Smrz, Vladimir, 39, 66
Socialism and Norris, 38, 55
Spangler, George, 80, 97, 111, 113
Spencer, Herbert, 100
Stein, Gertrude, 12, 44
Stevenson, Robert Louis, 26, 81
Stowe, *Uncle Tom's Cabin*, 38
Style in Norris's novels, 23, 36, 44,
  48-9

Tompkins, Juliet Wilbur, 34, 58
Twain, *Huckleberry Finn*, 66, 120

Walcutt, Charles Childe, 10, 21,
  22, 45, 48, 121
Walker, Franklin (biographer of
  Norris), 2, 4, 8, 12, 13, 16, 17,
  20-1, 22, 25-6, 27-8, 29-30, 31,
  32, 33, 34, 36, 39, 57, 72, 101,
  103, 109, 119, 122
Wilde, Oscar, 9
Wilson, Woodrow, 123
"Wise old man" archetype, 61

Yin and Yang, 2, 11, 56, 63, 64,
  95, 120

Ziff, Larzer, 8, 14, 23, 44, 48, 72,
  74, 80, 91, 120
Zola, Emile, 3, 6, 8, 13, 19, 20, 21,
  26, 28, 30, 33, 39, 43, 44, 45, 47-
  8, 49, 50, 51, 53, 64, 65, 79, 95,
  98, 111
    as mentor of Norris, 3, 20

MODERN AMERICAN LITERATURE
New Approaches

Yoshinobu Hakutani, General Editor

The books in this series deal with many of the major writers known as American realists, modernists, and post-modernists from 1880 to the present. This category of writers will also include less known ethnic and minority writers, a majority of whom are African American, some are Native American, Mexican American, Japanese American, Chinese American, and others. The series might also include studies on well-known contemporary writers, such as James Dickey, Allen Ginsberg, Gary Snyder, John Barth, John Updike, and Joyce Carol Oates. In general, the series will reflect new critical approaches such as deconstructionism, new historicism, psychoanalytical criticism, gender criticism/feminism, and cultural criticism.

For additional information about this series or for the submission of manuscripts, please contact:

Peter Lang Publishing
Acquisitions Department
516 N. Charles St., 2nd Floor
Baltimore, MD 21201